CAMBRIDGE LIBRARY COLLECTION

Books of enduring scholarly value

Cambridge

The city of Cambridge received its royal charter in 1201, having already been home to Britons, Romans and Anglo-Saxons for many centuries. Cambridge University was founded soon afterwards and celebrates its octocentenary in 2009. This series explores the history and influence of Cambridge as a centre of science, learning, and discovery, its contributions to national and global politics and culture, and its inevitable controversies and scandals.

A Descriptive Catalogue of the Manuscripts in the Library of Jesus College

M. R. James (1862-1936) is probably best remembered as a writer of chilling ghost stories, but he was an outstanding scholar of medieval literature and palaeography, who served both as Provost of King's College, Cambridge, and as Director of the Fitzwilliam Museum, and many of his stories reflect his academic background. His detailed descriptive catalogues of manuscripts owned by colleges, cathedrals and museums are still of value to scholars today. This volume contains James's catalogue of the manuscript holdings of Jesus College and will be welcomed by librarians and researchers alike.

Cambridge University Press has long been a pioneer in the reissuing of out-of-print titles from its own backlist, producing digital reprints of books that are still sought after by scholars and students but could not be reprinted economically using traditional technology. The Cambridge Library Collection extends this activity to a wider range of books which are still of importance to researchers and professionals, either for the source material they contain, or as landmarks in the history of their academic discipline.

Drawing from the world-renowned collections in the Cambridge University Library, and guided by the advice of experts in each subject area, Cambridge University Press is using state-of-the-art scanning machines in its own Printing House to capture the content of each book selected for inclusion. The files are processed to give a consistently clear, crisp image, and the books finished to the high quality standard for which the Press is recognised around the world. The latest print-on-demand technology ensures that the books will remain available indefinitely, and that orders for single or multiple copies can quickly be supplied.

The Cambridge Library Collection will bring back to life books of enduring scholarly value across a wide range of disciplines in the humanities and social sciences and in science and technology.

A Descriptive Catalogue of the Manuscripts in the Library of Jesus College

Montague Rhodes James

Cambridge University Press

CAMBRIDGE UNIVERSITY PRESS

Cambridge New York Melbourne Madrid Cape Town Singapore São Paolo Delhi

Published in the United States of America by Cambridge University Press, New York

www.cambridge.org
Information on this title: www.cambridge.org/9781108003513

This edition first published 1895
This digitally printed version 2009

ISBN 978-1-108-00351-3

A DESCRIPTIVE CATALOGUE

OF THE

MANUSCRIPTS

IN THE LIBRARY OF

JESUS COLLEGE, CAMBRIDGE

London: C. J. CLAY AND SONS,
CAMBRIDGE UNIVERSITY PRESS WAREHOUSE,
AVE MARIA LANE.
Glasgow: 263, ARGYLE STREET.

Leipzig: F. A. BROCKHAUS.
New York: MACMILLAN AND CO.

A

DESCRIPTIVE CATALOGUE

OF THE

MANUSCRIPTS

IN THE LIBRARY OF

JESUS COLLEGE, CAMBRIDGE

BY

MONTAGUE RHODES JAMES, LITT.D.,

FELLOW OF KING'S COLLEGE, CAMBRIDGE; DIRECTOR OF THE FITZWILLIAM MUSEUM

LONDON:
C. J. CLAY AND SONS,
CAMBRIDGE UNIVERSITY PRESS WAREHOUSE,
AVE MARIA LANE.
1895

Cambridge:
PRINTED BY J. AND C. F. CLAY,
AT THE UNIVERSITY PRESS.

REVERENDO · VIRO

D · GERMANO · MORIN

O · S · B

AMORIS · ERGO

PREFACE.

THE kindness of the Master and Fellows of Jesus College enables me to lay before the public for the first time a Catalogue of the Manuscripts belonging to the College. The only previous attempt is a list of seven volumes in Thomas James's *Ecloga Oxonio-Cantabrigiensis* (1600, p. 137): reprinted by Bernard in 1697: there is also a brief note in Halliwell's *Manuscript Rarities of the University of Cambridge* (1841, p. 173). Uffenbach (*Merkwürdige Reisen*, iii. 75) was unable to obtain access to the manuscripts.

The collection is mainly the gift of one donor, Thomas Man (B.A. 1674, M.A. 1678, M.D. 1687), Fellow of the College, and Vicar of Northallerton (see no. 8). More than fifty manuscripts were given by him, and a majority of these came from Durham Priory. Other northern monasteries, e.g. Hexham, Rievaulx, and Kirkstall, are also represented. Though not containing anything of surpassing importance, the collection is an interesting one enough. There is little good illuminated work, save in one Bible (no. 11). The Medical MSS. are fairly numerous. Probably the most attractive items in the Library are the early fragments in no. 5, the English passages in no. 13, the palimpsest Anglo-Saxon Homilies in no. 15, the Bury *Formulae* (no. 18), a French hymn (no. 21), the Psalter (no. 23), the Priscian (no. 28), the Rievaulx Catalogue (no. 34), the French *Lapidaire* (no. 44[1]), the Story of the Death of Judas (no. 46), the Wycliffite Gospels and New Testament (nos. 30, 47), the Obituary Roll in no. 55, Lydgate and

[1] This *Lapidaire* does not correspond with any of the texts printed by M. L. Panier in the *Bibliothèque des Hautes Études*.

Cato (no. 56), a list of books in no. 57, and the Chronicles (no. 58). As a specimen of writing, the volume by the scribe Emylton (no. 70) is very noteworthy.

On the remarkable and beautiful room in which the manuscripts are preserved, the reader should consult Willis and Clark's *Architectural History of the University of Cambridge* (ii. 165, iii. 460).

I should like, in conclusion, to express my particular obligations to the Librarian of the College, the Rev. F. J. Foakes-Jackson, who has been most kind in affording me access to the manuscripts under his charge.

M. R. JAMES.

CATALOGUE OF MANUSCRIPTS.

1. Q. A. I.

DECRETALES NOVAE GLOSSATAE.

Vellum, $15\frac{3}{4} \times 10$, ff. 208, text in double columns of 49 lines each, surrounded by gloss. Cent. xiii. Binding, original boards recovered: formerly had two clasps. Given by Mr Man, 21 Jan. 1685. At the beginning are two fly-leaves of a Canon Law MS. in double columns (xiii, xiv).

Collation: i^2 ii^2 a^{10}–d^{10} e^{10} (+ 7* *judicis*) f^{10}–m^{10} n^{12} o^{10}–r^{10} s^6 (+ slip) || A^{12} B^{12} C^6 (5 cancelled).

Provenance: Durham: on the top of the fourth fly-leaf has been an inscription of which only *Decretales* survives, and another partly cut off:

> Iste liber accomodat ...
> Omilium (? Dunlm) per dompnum Robertum de ...
> Quem si aliquis alienauerit anathe(ma sit).

On f. I. dunelm. E.

In the *Catt. Vett.* (of 1391)[1] p. 47, is this entry:

E. Decretales Nouae glo. II. fo. textus "et unitas in natura." These are the opening words of f. 2 in this MS.

Contents:

I. Incipit compilacio Gregorii ix. Prologue . . . . . f. I
c. I. de summa trinitate & fide catholica liber primus.

The first words of the gloss are gone.

The Collection is in five books.

[1] *Catalogi Veteres librorum Dunelm.:* Surtees Society, 1838.

2. A tract in a different and later hand, in double columns of 63 lines . . . . A 1
Inc. Legitur in Ezechiele venter tuus comedet et viscera tua implebuntur.

It is another compilation of Canon Law: references to the former are given at the end of each section.

On a fly-leaf at the beginning are three extracts in a xivth or xvth cent. hand, two from the Ottobonian Constitutions, and one from the Clementine.

2. Q. A. 2.

RUBRICA DE PROBATIONIBUS ETC. PER ANDREAM SICULUM.

Paper, $13\frac{1}{2} \times 9$, ff. 340, double columns of 43 to 63 lines. Cent. xv. Binding, plain wooden boards; covering, back and clasps gone.

Collation: a^{10} b^{6} c^{10} d^{6} (5 gone: 4, 6 blank) e^{10}–g^{10} h^{20} || i^{10} k^{6} l^{10}–s^{10} t^{4} v^{10}–z^{10} aa^{10} (9, 10 blank, gone) bb^{10} cc^{10} dd^{4} ee^{10}–mm^{10} nn^{8} (8 blank, gone).

The writing is almost certainly Italian and is rough and ugly: the initials are not added.

Incipit. CONTINUATUR SIC. visum est de confessionibus per quas aduersarius releuatur ab onere probandi.

On l. 4 is a marginal note ending V*ersus* fr. Alcok.

On the lower margin of q 10 *b* is the interesting stichometric note: In isto quinterno sunt pecie due colu*m* septe*m* linee. The columns here are of 63 lines, averaging 30 or 31 letters each. Quires y–mm are backed and guarded in the middle by strips of a MS. of cent. x. The earlier quires have guards from a xivth cent. MS. On the last cover is scribbled: Doctor alcok.

3. Q. A. 3.

BIBLIA SACRA.

Vellum, $13 \times 9\frac{1}{4}$, ff. 352 + 4, double columns of 54 lines each. Cent. xiii. Binding of cent. xviii. This MS. is no. 1 in T. James's *Ecloga Cantabrigiensis*, 1600, p. 137.

Collation: b^{12}–p^{12} (+ 2) q^{12}–z^{12} aa^{12}–gg^{12}.

The first quire is gone: the text begins in Gen. xxxvi. 24. patris sui. habuitque filium disan.

The order of the books is as follows:

Gen.—2 Chr.
Esdre I. = Ezra.
Uerba Neemie filii Esdre (running-title Esdre I.) = Nehemiah.
Esdre II. = 4 Esdr. i. ii. + 3 Esdr. + 4 Esdr. iii.–xvi. The books are joined without any note, thus:

Vade et annuncies populo meo qualia et quanta mirabilia domini dei uidisti. Et egit iosias pascha, etc.[1]———et coadunati sunt omnes in ierusalem iocundari secundum dispositionem domini dei israel. Anno • xxx° • ruine ciuitatis ierusalem.

Tobit—Psalms.

The Psalter shows more traces of wear than the rest of the book: at the end of it is a stichometric note: Expliciunt psalmi c. l. qui continent uersus numero quinque milia.

Isaiah—Malachi.
1, 2 Maccabees.
Prov.—Ecclus.
Matt.—Apoc.

The Eusebian Canons in a plain frame of yellow occupy two pages after the Apocalypse.

On the fly-leaves are two xvth century lists of the Books of the Bible.

4. Q. A. 4.

Summa Bartholomaei de Pisis de Casibus Iuris.

Vellum, 13 × 9, ff. 248, double columns of 36 to 47 lines. Cent. xv. Binding modern, leather over boards: clasps gone. This is no. 4 in James's list of MSS. at Jesus College, in his *Ecloga Cantabrigiensis*, 1600, p. 137.

Collation: a^8 (1, 2 cancelled) b^8–r^8 s^6 t^8–x^8 || i^8 ii^8 || y^8 z^8 || $\&^8$ 9^8 1^8 (wants 1) 2^8 (wants 1) 3^8 4^8 (wants 1) 5^8 (wants 8, blank).

The signatures *s* 5, 6 are marked *s ante finale, s finale.* After x occur two quires unsigned without interruption of text.

The writing is fairly good, probably English: the initials plain red and blue for the most part.

[1] This is C. 7 in Bensly's list of MSS. of 4 Esdras. *Missing Fragments* p. 42.

The work is an Encyclopaedia of Canon Law with a Prologue beginning Quoniam ut ait Gregorius super Ezechielem. It runs from *abbas* to *zelus*.

On the last cover is:

Caucio domini thome low et habet supplementum viz.
Auecen*n*am' super me*taphysi*cam cum aliis.

5. Q. A. 5.

PETRI COMESTORIS
HISTORIA SCHOLASTICA.

Vellum, 13 × 9½, ff. 152, double columns of 50 lines. Cent. xiii, xiv. Binding of cent. xviii. Probably identical with no. 5 in James's list, *Ecloga Cant.* p. 137. *Historia Egesippi, uti uidetur.*

Collation: i^8–xix^8.

There are two tattered fly-leaves from an early Missal (cent. x, xi) with 29 lines on a page, in a fine hand.

1 *a* has part of the Gospel for the Decollation of S. John Baptist (29 Aug.) and Graduals, etc. (neumes are given over the opening words).

1 *b*. Lectio Libri Sapientiae (Justorum animae).

2 *a*. Preface for S. Ypolitus (12 Aug.). Communion, *Dico autem uobis*. Collect for S. Eusebius, Conf. (14 Aug.). Epistle, *Testificor*. Gradual, *Os iusti*. Ant., *Iustus non con*. Euang., *Uigilate ergo*. r̄ r̄ (require reliqua ?) in nat. sc̄i marcelli .xvii. kl. Febr. in fol. Offi., *Desiderium anime*.

2 *b*. Assumptio S. Marie, two Collects and Lessons from Wisdom, *In omnibus requiem quesiui*.

The text is well written, with red and blue initials of pen-work. It ends in the chapter *de dyonisio areopagita. uolui uos reuocare ab impietate*.

It has suffered from damp in the upper margins.

6. Q. A. 6.

DECRETALES NOVAE GLOSSATAE.

Vellum, 13½ × 9½, ff. 269, double columns of text of varying length (46 lines), surrounded by gloss. Cent. xiii, xiv. Rebound. Two clasp-marks remain on the leaves. Given by Mr Man.

Closely resembles Q. A. 1. Fly-leaves (2) from a xiiith cent. MS. of Law in double columns.

Collation: i^{8} ii^{6} || a^{12}–h^{12} i^{10} k^{12} l^{12} m^{12+1} n^{12}–p^{12} q^{8} r^{8} s^{8+1} t^{12} v^{2} x^{10} y^{12} z^{12} (1 cancelled).

Provenance: Durham. On f. 14 *b* is the letter M. On 15 *a* is

M. Decretales gloss. de communi libraria monachorum dunelm.

The second leaf of the text (f. 16) begins *quemadmodum in canonica.* I cannot find the volume in the old Catalogues.

On the lower margin of f. 15 *a*, in a late xvth cent. hand, is:

a/16 (1) Inicium cuiuslibet capituli in hoc libro decretalium cum summulis et notulis eorundem.

(2) Decretales glosatae.

(3) Constitutiones noue duo innocencij iiii[ti], incomplete.

(4) Constitutiones alexandri iiii[ti].

(5) Expositio super i[d] c *debent superioribus* et libro vj prout concernit visitationem episcopi dunelm et conuentus dunelm.

(6) liber vj[tus] non glo(satus).

This table of contents seems complete.

(1) Is in a fine hand. The opening words of each chapter are given in a narrow column, and a line of note or summary added . . . . f. 1

f. 13 *b* is blank: on 14 *a* are 38 hexameters with interlinear gloss, giving the contents of the chapters. The first is:

Trinus • constituit • res • consue • postulat • elec •

On 14 *b* is another table of chapters.

(2) Text and gloss of the *Decretales Gregorii Noni* 15

Inc. Gregorius episcopus seruus seruorum dei.

Book v. ends on f. 218 *a*: the verso is blank.

(3) Begins on f. 219 *a*.

Statuimus ut signis eleccioni 219

Glossed.

(4) In three columns on a page, unglossed . . . . 221 *b*

(3) Resumed: begins imperfectly

ū in multis iuris articulis 225

Glossed: double columns.

f. 231 *a* blank: ff. 231 *b*, 232 *a* have later notes and constitutions of Boniface VI.

(6) Book vi. of the Decretals (Boniface VIII. 1298), in another hand, with table of chapters.

Text begins on 233

(5) Decretalis bonifacii in vi[to] libro.

Prouide attendentes.

De legatis uel clericis in aliena diocesi recipiendis . 269 *b*

7. Q. A. 7.

REPERTORIUM JURIS.

Paper, $12\frac{1}{8} \times 8\frac{1}{4}$, ff. 694 (including fragments), double columns, of 37 lines each. Cent. xv (late).

Collation: a^{12} (wants 1)–c^{12} d^{14} e^{12}–l^{12} m^{16} n^{16} o^{12}–s^{12} t^{12} (11, 12 cancelled) v^{12}–z^{12} || aa^{12}–ee^{12} ff^{18} gg^{6} (6 cancelled) hh^{12}–oo^{12} pp^{18} qq^{14} (14 cancelled) rr^{12} ss^{12} tt^{14} vv^{12}–zz^{12} A^{10} B^{12} C^{14} D^{12}–F^{12} G^{12} (6, 7 gone) H^{12} I^{12} K^{12} (2 gone) L^{10} (all except 1 imperfect).

It is a dictionary of Canon Law running from *Ab* (*Abbas*) to *Zelus*. The first article in B is *Babilon* and in C, *Calcar*. The writing is rough and the whole volume ugly. There is a vellum fly-leaf at the beginning.

8. Q. A. 8.

ISIDORI ETYMOLOGIARUM LIBRI XX.

Vellum, $11\frac{1}{4} \times 7\frac{3}{4}$, ff. 212, 40 lines to a page. Cent. xv. Written in England: modern binding. Given by Mr Man. Has the name Thomas Sandford, 1535: and Thomas Man, Vicarius de North Allerton.

Collation: a^{12}–r^{12} s^{6} t^{2} (blank).

The first words of f. 2 are: quam contempsisti postulantem.

The provenance is not clear: I do not find the volume in the Durham Catalogue.

The ornaments and initials at the beginnings of the books are exceedingly good and characteristic English work: blue, pink, green, orange, and gold are prominent colours.

9. Q. A. 9.

BIBLIA SACRA.

Vellum, $11\frac{3}{4} \times 7\frac{1}{2}$, ff. 241, double columns of 42 lines each. Cent. xv. Ex dono Caleb Pott (or Pett) hujus Coll. Alumni A° N^{s} C^{i} CIↃIↃCLXXVIII (1678).

Collation: thirty quires of eights: of the 31st the first leaf only is left.

Contents:

The Epistle to the Laodicenes follows Colossians on f. 193 *b*.

There are borders and initials of rough English work at the beginnings of the books: only in a few cases are they illustrative. The book of Jonah has a ship and a fish in the initial and that of the Acts a dove.

10. Q. A. 10.

Ps. Chrysostomi Opus Imperfectum in Matthaeum.

Vellum, $11\frac{3}{4} \times 8\frac{1}{4}$, ff. 158, in double columns of 48 lines each. Cent. xv. Binding: original boards rebacked and recovered; formerly fastened with two clasps: chain-mark at bottom inner corner of obverse board. At each end are four leaves of a service-book in double columns (of cent. xv) containing the office for Advent, with music on a four-line stave.

On the lower margin of one of the leaves at the end is:

Iste liber constat M. Willelmo Carlyll.

On fol. p 4 *b* at the end of homily 51 is: quod saxylby.

Collation: a^{10}–m^{10} n^{8} o^{8} p^{8} q^{8} (wants 6, 7) r^{10} (9, 10 cancelled).

On q 5 *b* is the note *hic deficit*, in Hom. 55: the page ends with *alterum non grauat*, the next begins *sed inde misericordiam christi.*

The writing is ugly and the initials of the plainest.

It is most probably this volume that appears in James's *Ecloga Cantabrigiensis*, p. 137, as no. 2, *Chrysostomus in opere imperfecto.*

11. Q. A. 11.

Biblia Sacra.

Vellum, 11⅛ × 7½, ff. 254, double columns of 60 lines each. Cent. xiii, 1290–1300, without donor's name.

Collation: I¹²–V¹² VI¹² (8 mutilated: one cancelled) VII¹² (wants 6: 2 Sam. i.) VIII¹² IX¹² X¹² (4, 5 gone: 2 Par. v.–xiii.) XI¹² (10, 11 gone: 3 Esdr. xviii.—Judith v. 7) XII¹² XIII¹² (4–7 gone: Ps. i.–xxxix.; 9 cancelled) XIV¹² (2, 3 gone: Ps. xcvii.–cxiii.; 7 mutilated: Prol. to Prov.) XV¹² XVI¹² (one cancelled after 6) XVII¹² XVIII¹² XIX¹² XX¹² (10, 11 gone: Joel ii. Am. i.–iii.) XXI¹² (5 gone: Zeph. Ag. i.) XXII¹² (12 gone: blank ?) XXIII¹² (1 gone: Matt. i.–iv.; 9 gone: Mark i.) XXIV¹² (2 cancelled, 12 gone).

Contents:

Genesis—2 Chron.
Esdras I. = Ezra.
Esdras II. = Nehemiah.
Esdras III. = 1 Esdr. *alias* 3 Esdr.
Judith, Tobias, Esther.
Job—Ecclus.
Isa. Jer. Lam. Baruch, Ezek.—Malachi.
i. ii. Maccabees.
Matt.—Luke xxii. 32–33, ut interficerentur. Et.

The writing is beautiful, the vellum very fine, and the historiated initials of more than usual interest. These last are as follows:

1. *Prol.* A tonsured ecclesiastic, in a monastic habit, as it seems, writing.
2. *Prol. to Genesis.* A dragon on the back of a nude man.
3. *Genesis.* Initial I, the length of the page, spreading out at the bottom and containing 16 pictures on gold grounds:

   1. Christ holding the divided globe. 2. Christ: water on *R.* 3. Christ: tree on *R.* 4. Christ: moon on *L.*, sun on *R.* 5. Christ: beasts on *R.* 6. Christ: Adam reclining on *R.* 7. Christ seated full-face, blessing. 8. The Fall; serpent has not, as often, a human head: Eve is on *R.* 9. Cain killing Abel. 10. The Ark: two-storied building in a ship. 11. A building falling: a man on *R.*: ? the tower of Babel. 12. Sacrifice of Isaac. Ram on *L.* 13. Annunciation: angel on *L.* 14. Christ full-face at column, scourged by two men. 15. The Crucifixion, with the Virgin and S. John: at the feet of Christ, outside the initial, is a monk in red over blue, kneeling on a footstool. 16. The Resurrection, Christ has bannered cross: two guards below. Grotesques: a monkey tilting at a man: both ride on dragons.

4. *Exodus.* Moses, horned, receives the tables from Christ, half-length, in a circle.

5. *Leviticus.* Three men: fire falls on them from a cloud. Nadab or Korah.

6. *Numbers.* Four Jews kneel on *L.*: in centre a calf on a low pillar: on *R.* Moses, horned, points to it, and prepares to let fall the tables.

7. *Deut.* A crowd of nine Jews led to *R.* over water by Moses, horned, with rod.

8. *Jos.* Joshua bearded, nimbed, and robed faces *L.* and holds up his hand toward the sun in a cloud. Four men on *R.* look *L.*

9. *Jud.* Four mailed men with surcoats: one with spear and green shield: Christ speaks out of a cloud.

10. *Ruth.* Above. Boaz with staff: below, Ruth stretches her hand up to it: below her, a reaper in close cap.

11. 1 *Sam.* Hannah, with Samuel, kneels, face *R.*, at altar with lamp above it: behind her, Elkanah and a youth with pitcher on shoulder.

2 *Sam.* Initial gone.

12. 1 *Kings.* Blue ground with red dots. A courtier presents Abishag to David crowned in bed.

13. 2 *Kings.* Red ground. A tower, with red ground: Ahaziah crowned falls headlong from it.

14. 1 *Chr.* Three seated men, one with book.

15. 2 *Chr.* Solomon kneels at altar with gold cross above it: an attendant behind him. Red ground, gold spots.

Prol. to Esdr. Has fine decorative initial.

16. 1 *Esdr.* Above, a king, with sword, seated: below, a queen with green apple or cup.

17. 2 *Esdr.* (*Neh.*). Under architecture, a man in cloak and tunic with bucket and aspergillum.

18. 3 *Esdr.* A youth (Zerubbabel) addressing a throned king with sceptre.

Judith. Initial gone.

19. *Tobias.* Tobit, blind, seated with hands out: on *R.*, Raphael winged and nimbed leads away the child Tobias: the dog follows.

20. *Esther.* Ahasuerus stretches down his sceptre to Esther crowned, kneeling below him. In the lower margin, Haman in tunic, blindfold and bound, hangs from the initial.

21. *Prol. to Job.* A Lion: fine.

22. *Job.* On *L.* his wife and a friend talk to Job, nude, seated.

23. (*Ps. lxviii.*) *Saluum me fac.* Above, two men paddling in a boat, face each other: below, Jonah, nude, emerges from the fish's mouth and clutches a tree on *R.*

24. *Exultate.* David seated plays on three bells. Above his head is an organ, below his feet is a harp. Gold ground.

25. *Prov.* On *R.* Solomon crowned, seated, with birch-rod: on *L.* in front Rehoboam seated, nude; behind him a tonsured youth with joined hands.

26. *Eccl.* On *L.* four men: in centre a pile of gold cups and plates: on *R.* Solomon sits and speaks.

27. *Cant.* The Virgin crowned, kissing the Child: seated.

28. *Wisd.* Solomon throned, hands a sword to a man on *L.*

29. *Ecclus.* Solomon throned, points upward to a cloud: four men kneel on *L.*

30. *Isaiah.* Isaiah nude, stands: his hands and feet are bound to the top and bottom of the initial: two men saw him from below with a frame-saw.

31. *Jer.* Jeremiah kneels on *R.* stoned by two men: one has a winged head-dress. Above the prophet's head is the Divine Hand.

32. *Lam.* Jeremiah on *L.* sits with hand to head: a falling city on *R.*

33. *Baruch.* A nimbed tonsured man writing.

34. *Ezek.* Above, the Evangelistic symbols: a wheel in the centre: below, Ezekiel sleeping, head to *L.*

35. *Prol. to Dan.* A crowned devil with human body and arms and four legs.

36. *Dan.* On *L.* Habakkuk, nimbed, carrying loaves in his robe and a bucket in his hand, is borne by an angel holding his hair: on *R.* Daniel standing in a tower-like building with four lions' heads on *R.* greets him.

37. *Hosea.* Gomer and another woman on *L.* addressed by Hosea nimbed seated on *R.*

38. *Joel.* Standing addresses four men seated on *R.* in peaked hats.

39. *Obad.* Under architecture, seated, addresses five seated men.

40. *Jonah.* Similar to no. 23.

41. *Micah.* Nimbed, seated and holding two branches.

42. *Nahum.* Beardless, nimbed, holds up his skirts and walks to *L.* On *R.* a small man standing in the door of a tower seems to mock him.

43. *Habakkuk.* Nimbed, sits and points to book: an angel speaks to him from above.

44. *Zechariah.* Above, a bust of the prophet: below, a king: below, a figure on a red horse, a white horse beyond him.

45. *Malachi.* Nimbed, slaughters a beast lying on an altar: the blood caught in a green bowl on a stem.

46. 1 *Macc.* Christ, nimbed, with cross-staff, in centre, face *R.* Behind him on *L.* a prostrate man and a mailed man with spear: on *R.* five seated people.

47. 2 *Macc.* On *L.* a stooping man holding a box emerges from a gate. Two mailed men with shields and raised swords are about to smite him.

48. *Luke.* Gold ground. Luke tonsured and beardless turns to *R.* and looks at his pen: he is writing on a scroll at a table across the picture. Below, a winged ox.

The drawing of these pictures is particularly fine: nos. 19, 41, 46 are excellent examples.

12. Q. A. 12.

CONSUETUDINES ORDINIS CARTHUSIENSIS.

Vellum, $10\frac{5}{8} \times 7\frac{1}{2}$, ff. 215, double columns of 30 lines. Cent. xv, xvi. Binding, original, stamped leather over boards: two stamps are used, one a small rose, the other lozenge-shaped containing a double eagle: this last dispersed rather irregularly over the cover. The name Richardus Petteward Suff. 1619, is on f. t 8.

Collation: A^8 B^8 || a^6 b^8–m^8 n^6 o^8 (1 cancelled) p^8–bb^8 cc^8 (4 cancelled, 6–8 blank, gone).

Contents:

Tabula super statuta noua et uetera . . . . A 1
Modus legendi statuta (later) . . . . B 8 *b*

Capitula prime partis consuetudinum ordinis carthusiensis . . .	a 1
Text	a 2
Capitula secunde partis	h 2
Text	h 2 *b*
Capitula (and text) tercie partis	n 6
Prima pars nouarum constitucionum (no title)	q 2
Secunda pars	r 6
Tercia pars	t 3
Tercia compilacio statutorum ord. Carthus. (in another and later hand)	v 1
Notes on accent and pronunciation	bb 2
Supplicatio from Will. Tynbych, Prior of the London Charterhouse in 1516, to the Franciscan Prior Major of the order, to be allowed a coadjutor	bb 3
Another, 1517	bb 3 *b*
De obseruatione festi S. Brunonis (1415) and other extracts from Carte generales questiones sent to the General Chapter by John Ingilbi, Prior of Sheen, 1494	bb 5
Other questions, supplications and responses, the last dated 1520.	

The writing is very good and clear: there is little or no decoration.

13. Q. A. 13.

SERMONES.

Vellum, $10\frac{1}{4} \times 7\frac{1}{2}$, ff. 210, varying number of lines to a page. Cent. xiv, xv. Original binding, white skin over boards: two clasps. Given by Mr Man.

Collation: a^{4} (1 gone) b^{12}–e^{12} f^{8} ‖ g^{8} h^{12} i^{12} ‖ k^{12}–s^{12} t^{12} (12 gone). Another (blank) quire cut out.

Provenance: probably Durham. On the fly-leaf is an entry of late xvth cent.

Sermones quorundam qui sic incipiunt
Missus est. 2° fo. ascendam.

A slip is cut out of the leaf; then follows:

N. Sermones de sancta maria.

ii. Sermones de sanctis et de tempore cum tabula: sermo de uisitacione non negligenda, etc.

Item sermones de tempore et sanctis cum tabula.

I do not find this book in the Catalogues.

Contents:

1. Sermons on the Virgin: in double columns of 44 lines.

The first page is damaged. It begins:

Flos de radice eius asscendet. Flos est christus.

On f. 2 *b* a second sermon, on *Missus est*, containing English verses, and a story about an image in the city Cyclopes, in India.

2. f. 4 begins with *Ascendam*. This is the first word of a sermon on S. Andrew. Ascendam in palmam et apprehendam fructum eius. The sermons are *de sanctis* from S. Andrew to S. Katherine, and are numbered from 62 to 126. There are two for S. Francis (one very long) and one for S. Clara.

3. Sermones de tempore.

Inc. Mitte agnum etc. ysa. xvi. In verbis prepositis ysayas.

They are numbered from 1 to 53.

A Table follows.

4. A sermon in single lines, 2½ pages, in another hand.

On *Fratres tuos visitatis*.

5. Sermons.

In double columns of 49 lines: foliated from 1 to 33.

Inc. Reuertar in principio cum Tobia. Thob. xij. *Reuertar ad eum qui misit me vos autem benedicite deum*.

6. Sermons, in another hand, 43 lines to a page: foliated 34 to 149.

Inc. De nocte surrexit. Prouerb. ult. Karissimi videtis quia quilibet homo componitur ex duobus.

The second sermon begins:

Ante quorum oculos Christus Ihesus proscriptus est.

This and several of the following sermons contain passages in English.

7. The five last pages contain a Table to this set of sermons, in another hand.

A specimen of the English (fol. 86 *b*) is:

Contrariam: Whan thou art wroth & wylt ham wreche
be holde the leere that I the teche
th(r)owygh myn ryth hand the nayl yt good
for ȝeef ther fore & be nowght wroth.

And f. 87: I haue in loue & freysch in mynde
the blod of hym that was so keende.

14. Q. A. 14.

BEDA SUPER GENESIM ET EXODUM.

Vellum, 11¼ × 8, ff. 154, 29 lines to a page. Cent. xii.

Given by Mr Man. Binding, original boards, covered with white skin, and fastened by strap and pin: the strap has its original perforated metal end, with rudely incised pattern.

Collation: i^{10}–vi^{10} vii^{8} viii^{10}–xi^{10} xii^{6} (3–6 cancelled) || i^{10} (1 cancelled) ii^{12} iii^{12} $iv^{?}$ (1 left).

Thc leaves attached to the binding at beginning and end are partially erased leaves of another copy of Bede on Genesis, having 34 lines to a page, of about the same date as the volume.

Provenance: Durham. On f. 1 *a* is:

A. Liber sancti Cuthberti de Dunelm.

The second leaf begins:

Potest autem non improbabiliter,

and on the top of the page is:

Beda super genesim usque cap. 21 tantum.

I cannot find this volume in the *Catalogi Veteres.*

The writing is beautiful: the commentary on Exodus is in another hand of the same date. There is a very fine initial I on f. 1 *b*, of green, red, and yellow, on blue, in the form of a ladder of conventional foliage.

On 1 *a* is: John Richardson's book pretium ijs vjd.

Contents:

Ends on Exod. xxvi. (Quos operies laminis aureis) with the words: et odio habens iniquitatem: pios nouerit.

15. Q. A. 15.

PETRI LOMBARDI SENTENTIARUM LIBRI IV.

Vellum, 11 × 7¾, ff. 132, mostly in double columns of 40 lines each. Cent. xi, xiv. Given by Mr Man, Jan. 21, 1685. Binding original: white skin over boards: strap and pin fastening.

Collation: i^{6} ii^{4} || a^{8} b^{8} c^{12} || d^{8} e^{8} f^{8} || g^{8} h^{8} i^{8} || k^{8} l^{8} m^{8} n^{12} (12 cancelled) || iii^{16} (7, 11, 12, 14, 15 cancelled), 132 leaves.

Provenance: Durham? The press-mark on f. 11 is Textus iiij^{or} libro*rum* *sententi*ar*um* E. The 2nd leaf of the text begins *pluralitatis non.*

It may be the copy entered thus in *Catt. Vett.* (pp. 22 and 98):

P. Textus Sententiarum cum Libro Penitentiae et aliis ii. fo., "pluralitatis."

Contents:

I. Quires i, ii, and iii (at end) are palimpsest: the older writing contains fragments of Homilies in Anglo-Saxon upon the Gospels, of cent. xi, xii, 27 lines to the page.

f. 1 remains intact.

Inc. Spa spa he him on Lífe belíet þaðahe clýpode opeorþan tohis ælmíhtígan fæder fæder mín íc pílle þæt þa pumon midme þeþinne fortgeaf of ðisum middan earde.

Ends on l. 1 of verso.

halgan gaste onanre godcundnýsse an aelmihtigod abutan ende. Amen.

LARSPELL (*rubr.*).

Laepde menn behofiað þæt him larpas secgan þagodspellican lare þe hi on bocum leornodon. John xiv. 23 is quoted.

f. 2 is palimpsest: the upper writing in double columns of 34 lines each, of cent. xiv, xv, very rude. At the top, *Assit principio S. Maria meo.*

Incipit paruulus tractatus de vii peticionibus...et vii vitiis capitalibus. Pater noster. Cum hec oracio a sapientissimo.

The lower writing is lost, save perhaps a line or two at the bottom, where galls have been applied.

On f. 3 *b* about five lines might be read.

f. 4 *a* is more than half free from later writing, but erased.

f. 4 *b* is erased, but mostly decipherable.

ff. 5 *a*–6 *b* erased, but almost all decipherable: the last seven lines on f. 6 *b* untouched: they refer to the text, He that exalteth himself shall be abased.

f. 7. A table to the Sentences. Cent. xiii, xiv. Only the faintest traces of the earlier writing appear. So with

f. 8, of which the *verso* is blank. f. 9 *a* is blank. 9 *b* is half covered with notes: the upper half of f. 10 is cut away. Possibly f. 10 might be deciphered.

In quire iii

f. 1 *a* is covered with miscellaneous notes.

ff. 1 *b*–3 *b* contain verses (cent. xiv), about 140 in number.

Peniteas cito peccator cum sit miserator
Iudex. et sunt hec quinque tenenda tibi.

End:

Plauso tartarei confusio multa ministri
Et fuga cohortum felix adopcio celi.

On all these leaves the old writing is hopelessly defaced.

ff. 4–9 *a* a tract, cent. xiv, xv, in double columns:

Cum summa teologice discipline diuiditur in duas partes.

ff. 4–7 are palimpsest: on 7 *b*, 8, 9 I can see nothing: 9 *b* is blank.

ff. 10, 11 are carefully scraped, but have no later writing.

On the last cover are traces of a page of the Anglo-Saxon.

II. Quires a–n contain the four books of the Sentences. They are well written, and rubricated, and have marginal notes in various hands.

16. Q. A. 16.

AUGUSTINI QUAEDAM.

Vellum, $11\frac{3}{4} \times 7$, ff. 130, double columns of 32 lines each. Cent. xii. Bound in two consecutive sheets of a Psalter (xiiith cent.) in double columns of 27 lines each, contains parts of the Psalms *Judica Domine* xxxiv.—*Dixi custodiam* xxxviii. and *Deus auribus* xliii.—*Deus deorum* xlix. Given by Mr Man: it has the name of Thomas Iveson 1567. In the binding is a bit of a xvth century table.

Collation: a^8–q^8 r^4 (3, 4 cancelled).

On the last leaf of l (f. 88 *b*) is the note ii. id*us* dec*embres*: on n^8 (104) xvi. kal. Aug. and another date, cut off, on the next page.

Provenance: perhaps Hexham or Rievaulx: on the fly-leaf is a xiith cent. table of the contents, and a xvth cent. press-mark.

Augustinus de baptismo et de natura et gracia et alia litera B.

The first words of f. 2 are consortium non accessissent.

The writing and initials (in blue, green and red) are both very good.

Contents:

17. Q. A. 17.

ALYSONI QUAESTIONES METAPHYSICAE.

Paper, $11\frac{1}{8} \times 7\frac{1}{2}$, ff. 212, 31 lines to a page. Cent. xv. Original binding of stamped leather over boards: clasp gone.

Collation: a^{12}–f^{12} g^{10} h^{12}–o^{12} p^{12} (11, 12 cancelled) q^{12}–s^{12}.

Quire q is partly in another and smaller hand.

Contents:

Questiones on Books i.–x. and xii. of Metaphysics.

On a fly-leaf is a table of the questions on Books i.–vii. At the end of Book x. is the note:

Incipit xii[us] quia super xi[o] non scripsit.

The volume is imperfect, ending in Book xii.

There is a short prologue addressed to a Pope, to whom the author dedicates his work. No name appears, but he speaks of himself as a Dominican.

Inc. Cum cetere sciencie ad cognicionem summi boni conferant, sanctissime pater.

The writing is ugly. On the fly-leaf is pencilled:

Richardus Hughes Bibliothecae Custos 1625 Doctore Magistro Andrews.

18. Q. B. 1.

FORMA COMPOSITIONUM CARTARUM, ETC.

Paper, $11\frac{5}{8} \times 8\frac{3}{4}$, ff. 273 and fragments, 37 lines to a page. Cent. xv.

Collation: ii^{14} iii^{16} $iiij^{16}$ v^{14} vj^{16}–ix^{16} || i^{12} ii^{12} (wants 11) iii^{12} $iiij^{12}$ v^{12} vj^{12} (wants 7–10) vij^{12} (wants 5, 11, 12) $viij^{12}$–xij^{12} $xiij^{12}$ (2 almost gone) xiv^{12} (3–12 almost gone).

Binding, red vellum on boards: strap and pin fastening: no chain mark. It is lettered on the back in black letter:

Forma Composicionum Cartarum Obligacionum Acquietanciarum Indenturarum Libellorum et Appellacionum cum alijs pro studio Abbatis.

A note on f. 1 says:

Scriptus videtur hic Liber in usum Abbatis S[cti] Edmundi de Bury.

The first quire is gone.

f. 1 begins:

quot pene rerum contrahendarum de quibus Curia Regia se non intromittet.

f. 2 *a*. Obligacio simplex.

S. P. de O. Dat. apud O. 10 Hen. IV.

Item aliter.

In the margin of f. 3 *a*, opposite to a form of bond, is written: 'viz. Acton Burnell.'

On f. 3 *a* is a form for an abbas Sc̄ī E.

3 *b*. W. prior de N(orwic) et eiusdem loci conuentus Norwic. dioc.

f. 7 *b* (added). Acquittance from Adam Cykow de Bury, Cordwainer, and his wife Helena to John Bernasse de Bury.

Indenture between W. N. Archd. Sudbury and Hugo Sandeby, parson of the Ely portion of West Walton.

Receipt by W. C. Cellarer of St E. de B. from J. N. Knight, through J. B. and J. D. his receivers at Chellesworth. 8 Hen. V.

Also from J. B. Rector of S. Laurence, Norwich.

8 *a*. Emma widow of K. B. quondam ciuis et Stok fissh monger of London receives from W. B. Capellanus of St E. de B. Given at S. Mary's Crokelane.

9 *a*. Official of Christianity at Oxford.

W. de N. sacrist of S. Edmund: J. Abbot.

9 *b*. J. Abbot of monastery of S. Bernard, O.S.B., Norwic. dioc.

10 *b* (added). Acquittance from W. Cellarer of S. Edmund to a tenant at Wanflet.

John Gedney, pitanciarius of S. E. de B., from Rich. Alred, for dn̄s Cham*ber* (?) hemgraue. 6 Hen. V.

ff. 11 sqq. *Literae attorniatoriae*.

12 *a*. J. B. Camerarius of Bury.

12 *b*. *Concessiones*.

John filius Regis Anglie, Dux Aquit. et Lanc. comes Lincoln. Leycestr. et Derb.

Manumissio by W. Abbot of S. E. de B., at request of Henry Prince of Wales, of Ed. Moket and his son Thomas. 10 Hen. IV.

13. Text continued.

13 *a*. *De literis procuratoriis*.

One of 1372.

14 *a*. One of 1374.

21 *a* margin. Quere literam abbatis de langley directa Abbati de Bury super excommunicacione et apostasia E. de B. ut asserunt et responcionem eiusdem abbatis de bury in libro traducionum figurato C. 65 fo. p^{o}.

23 *b* margin. Quere aliud mandatum pro magistro scolarum postea fol. $\overset{xx}{\text{iiij}}$ xv viz. vij^{o} fol. ante casus excommunicacionis et vide pro scolis adulterinis infra libertatem eandem (?) in isto folio cuius principium est ex alia parte folij.

32. Wills dated 1403 and 1399.

34. *De citacionibus*.

59. *De sentencijs diffinitiuis*.

60 *b*. A sentence dated 1295 (Prioress of K.).

64 *b*. *De satisfaccionibus*.

68. *De commissionibus*.

70. *De testibus*.

77. *De eleccionibus*.

83. I. de Kyrkeby Ep. Elyens. Alan de W. Prior Elyens.

87 *b*. Election of Alan de Walsingham. 1341.

110 *a*. Laus tibi sit christe quia liber terminat iste.

110 *b*. Constitution of Th. Arundell Abp Cant.

Constitution of H. Chychille Abp Cant.

111. Licencia dandi siluam de bradfeld sencler (Bradfield S. Clair) ad manum mortuam. To Abbot of Bury.

Tho. Skoston Chiualer, Will. Gascoyne, Rad. Chaumberleyn, Joh. Broke, parson of Polstede, Edm. Carleton, Joh. Rookwoode, Joh. Lawney, Rich. Storesacr. are mentioned. 5 Hen. ?.

Probate of will sec. formam Ecclesie de Bury, before Symon, Sacrist.

111 *b*. Protestacio bona pro exempt.

Marg.: a° d[i] m° cc° lxiij°.

Protestacio Symonis Ep. Norwyc. de iurisdiccione exempcionis S. Edmundi e libro tradicionum figurato C. 65[1]. Item alia protestacio Roberti Ep. Archilioñ suffraganei henrici Ep. Norwyc. facta a. d. m° ccc° lxxj° et protest. Iohannis paschalis Ep. Suffr. Willelmi Ep. Norwyc. facta a. d. m° ccc° xliiij° et protest. Rolandi Armachani Archiep. Suffr. Will. Ep. Norwyc. facta a. d. m° ccc° xxxv°: omnes iste patent in dicto libro tradicionum pariter in vno folio et similiter in r° thos.

Quere aliam protest. factam per K. de Casteñ et causam factam tempore quo Ricardus abbas fuit in arcis constituta propter violenciam penarum absque consensu ca[i] concederet potita in libro tradicionum intitulato C. 65 fol. se*x*to.

112. Processus factus per papam contra regem anglie pro occupacione bonorum cardinalium.

Ventrem suum dolet.

113 *b*. Interdictum communitatis ville Oxon. 1354.

118 *b*. Acquittance from Robert (?) Prior of Norwich and William Prior of S. Mary's Butley, 1417: to Prior and Convent of Bury.

119 *b*. John Gedney (pitanciarius of Bury) to Will. Reyner of Wirlyngton iuxta Mildenhale. 5 Hen. V.

120 *a*. William Abbot of Bury to Will. Comes of Bradefeld monachorum. 10 Hen. V.

121 *a*. Alienacio medietatis personatus Eccl. de ffresyngfelde. Henry ... to Abbot of Bury: Symon ffylbeig Chiualer, Roger Perrat clerk, Walter Banyes, John Alderford.

122 *b*. Margaret Prioress of S. George, Thedford, concedes a messuage in Mustowe Street, Bury, to John Cole of Bury: formerly the property of Osbert Otewy: Will. Gatele of Thetford, John Maggys, and Thos byng of Bury. 7 Hen. V.

123 *b*. *Appeals.*

125 *a*. Ad mea principia sis deprecor alma maria.

Quoniam sub pena excommunicacionis.

132. *Expliciunt sentencie late in corpore decretalium.*

Incipiunt sentencie late in corpore decretorum.

143 *a* (blank). Watermark, a two-legged dragon with horns.

143 *b*. Charters concerned with Bardwell.

148 (1st of a quire). Assit principio sancta maria meo.

Numquid comes bannitus. The text is *Dubia et solutiones.*

[1] This is a Consuetudinary now in the possession of H.H. Prince Frederick Duleep Singh.

159 *b*. Remember that I owe you iij d ob. for Lace. Goldingham (xv, xvi).
167 *b* blank. Libro vij.
168 *a*. *Abbates seruiuntur* hic per Jo vel sic.
174 *b* blank.
190 *a* blank.
190 *b*. Formulae recommence.
191 *b* blank. Scribbled.
192. Dudum communitas sic. At top 'Mey.'
De sepulturis in vij^{mo}.
196 *b* blank.
197 *a*. *De homicidio in antiquis.*
201 *a*. Assit principiis sancta maria meis.
Liber vi^{tus}.
Prohemium sixti libri.

This is the last division of the book. A commentary on the sixth book of *Decreta*. *De electionibus*, *de tempore ordinandi*, etc.

The fly-leaves are from one or two unfinished musical service books (xiv, xv). That at the beginning has antiphons for the Assumption. Those at the end have proses with music in three parts on a 5-line stave.

...trarum ab hoste nescio. fit hic prouisio in hoc adiutorium felix audicio.

f. 1. Si mundus uiueret mundus pecunia regnarente inter nos pax et concordia sed cum debilitet nos auaricia plantat et inserit lites et odia duce discordia.

Verso. Fas et nephas ambulant fere passu pari | prodigus non redimit uicium auari | uirtus temperancia quadam singulari | debet medium ad utrumque uicium caute contemplari.

Leuiter ex merito ferendum quod patimur meremur.

f. 2 *a*. (Ponti)fex egregie | decus cleri | speculum ecclesie | patrie solacium | tuorum refugium | fac rogamus | ut cernamus | iudicem propicium.

Ue ... fides geniti purgauit crimina ...

Verso unfinished.

f. 3 *a*. -mium ne recepto premio declinent obsequium sed quo plus suspenditur plus uenturum uenditur noto longo uenditum perdit munus meritum. M.

Crucifigat oneris: verso attached to cover.

There can be no doubt that the MS. belonged to the Abbot of Bury.

19. Q. B. 2.

FORMULARUM LIBER.

Paper, $11\frac{1}{4} \times 7\frac{1}{2}$, ff. 165 and fragments, 41 lines to a page. Cent. xv, xvi.

Binding: a piece of otter's skin, measuring $22\frac{1}{2} \times 11\frac{1}{2}$, with the hair still on it: formerly fastened with a strap.

Formerly belonged to John (?) Watson of Blith; Edmund Clyfton of Aula Regia Cantabr.; Rob. Cressy, LL.B., official of the Archdeacon of Nottingham. The last may have given it to the College. The name Robert Palmer also occurs. The paper leaves are enclosed in a sheet of parchment, of which the last half is gone. On the remaining leaf, in a rude frame, is the inscription

Orate pro anima Johannis (?) Watson de Blida qui istum librum fieri fecit ad vsum ecclesie parochialis de Blida qui obiit tercio kalend... Augusti anno domini millesimo ccccmo ...o cuius anime propicietur deus Amen.

Collation: a^{14} b^{14} (wants 14) c^{14} (wants 12, 13: 3 is loose) d^{8} (wants 3) e^{22} (15–21 gone) f^{16} (wants 15) (g gone?) h^{8}: then ten loose and torn leaves: i^{8} (wants 5–8) k^{8} (wants 3 and 8) l^{12} (wants 1–8 and 12) m^{12} (wants 11, 12) n^{12} (wants 2, 3) o^{12} p^{16} (wants 12) q^{14} (3 gone, 14 nearly gone).

Contents:

20. Q. B. 3.

Summa de Vitiis.

Vellum, $11 \times 7\frac{1}{4}$, ff. 142, double columns of 40 lines each. Cent. xiv, xv. In an ugly hand. Given by Mr Man.

Binding: pasteboard, covered externally with a sheet of a large Psalter of cent. xiii, in double columns of 27 lines each. The text begins in Ps. lxvii. (Exsurgat deus) and ends in Ps. lxx. The Psalm *Saluum me fac* has a rather bold initial. The insides of the covers are lined with other pieces as it seems of the same book, but at each end of the volume a sheet of a xvth cent. index to a Canon Law book is pasted over them.

Collation: a^{12}–l^{12} m^{10}.

Provenance: ? Durham: fol. 2 begins *Indifferenter tamen.* I do not find it in *Catt. Vett.*

Contents:

1.	Summa de vitiis	f. 1
2.	Tractatus de virtutibus	87 *b*

No. 1 begins: Primo videndum est quid sit peccatum.

It ends on 87 *a*. There are a good many marginal notes, from which, rather than from the text itself (which has a late look), I conclude the date to be the xivth century. At the end is: Expl. summa de vitiis.

No. 2. f. 87 *b*. Postquam dictum est de morbis ipsius anime.

Ends f. 142 *a*: pauci in virginitate. Expl. de uirtutibus.

21. Q. B. 4.

PSALTERIUM.

Vellum, $10\frac{1}{8} \times 7\frac{3}{8}$, ff. 96, 25 lines to a page. Cent. xiii.

No donor's name. Binding: boards covered with parchment: modern label.

Collation: i^2 (2 cancelled) a^{10}–c^{10} d^8 e^{10}–g^{10} h^{10} (+ 9* *omnes sancte virgines*) i^{10} k^6.

Contents:

On f. 1 *a* is a hymn (cent. xiii) in French, in 7 stanzas of 6 lines each:

Ave ihu ki p*or* n*ou*s pecheurs del cel descendistis
E de la ui*r*gine marie char e sanc preistes
E u*os*tre seinte deite de deuz sun cors cuueristes
Ke deus esteis e creatur uerai hume deuenistes
Sauue la ui*r*ginite de la seinte pucele nasquistes
E par la porte close del bonure uentre issistes.

Each stanza begins with Ave ihu. A rubric follows:

Ki ces saluz suuent dirat: ia ben del cel ne lui faudrat.
De ses pechez pardun au*er*at: e a p*re*s sa fin a deu irat.
Ke n*os*tre sire le otreat a seint franchiff ke les rimat.

On the same page is a *Memoria* of S. Sebastian (xv cent.).

Also in red: Iste liber Pertinet Thome Bryston (xvi) and also the name Thomas Thomylthorp (xvii).

On f. 1 *b* is a long hymn in two columns; 16 stanzas of 12 lines each (xiiith cent.).

Iesu princeps maiestatis }
Fons perhennis pietatis } angelorum domine,
Qui de celis descendisti }
Atque nasci uoluisti } ex maria uirgine.
Ad te pie mi saluator }
Gemens clamat hic peccator } sub peccati pondere,
Pande sinum pietatis }
Vt trementem pro peccatis } digneris suscipere.

The Psalter.

The words *Beatus uir—impiorum* are in blue and red capitals, ornamented. The Collects are appended to each Psalm. The following Psalms have large initials: nonc are figured.

Dominus illuminatio.	Exultate.
Dixi custodiam.	Cantate (a good design).
Quid gloriaris.	Domine exaudi (Ps. ci. *lat.*).
Dixit insipiens.	Dixit dominus.
Saluum me fac.	

Ps. cli. *Pusillus eram*, with the Collect *Deus exaudibilis*, follows Ps. cl.

The Litany has been very oddly treated. The original names of the Saints invoked after Sc̄e Clemens have been rewritten in the xvth century, and extended to the full Sarum form for the days of the week. This has necessitated the insertion of an extra leaf, f. 9* of quire h: the verso of f. 78 being entirely palimpsest. The original list of Saints ended at f. 78 *a*, col. 2, 3 lines from the bottom: the Saints now occupy the whole of f. 78 and col. 1 of f. 79. It is not possible at present to determine the original names.

The Sequences on f. 81 sqq. have musical notes on a 4-line stave for the first verse of each. There are two for S. Augustine, *Magne pater Augustine* and *Celi ciues applaudite*, which indicate that the book was for use in an Augustinian house.

On f. 95 *b* is the poem:

Virgo gaude digna laude templum sancti spiritus.
Que nature uicto iure concepisti celitus.

In 68 ll.

Then follow 7 lines:

Gaude uirgo gloriosa uerbum uerbo concepisti
Gaude tellus fructuosa uite fructum protulisti.

The fly-leaf at the end is from a Missal of cent. xiii, in double columns of 30 lines each, containing Proper Prefaces for Easter, etc.

22. Q. B. 5.

GRADUALE ECCLESIAE DUNELMENSIS CUM NOTIS.

Vellum, $11\frac{1}{2} \times 6\frac{3}{4}$, ff. 139 + 3, 8 lines of music to a page. Cent. xiv, xv.

Binding: wooden boards, with later leather back, clasp gone. Given by Mr Man.

Collation: i^2 (1 cancelled) a^{12}–l^{12} m^6 (+6*): 2 fly-leaves at end.

Graduals and Tracts for the year.

On the fly-leaf at the beginning, in a later hand, are two Tracts or Graduals:

Desiderium anime eius tribuisti
Qui Lazarum. Requiem eternam.

At the top of a page (in the Palm Sunday service) in a xvith century hand is:

Will still to wiffe woulde leade me
But wit would ytt a red me
Off wyving to be were
Inne Will to Will in wivinge
Or elles farewell all thryving,
Awoue ytt well I dere. I. C.

On the first page of the *Proprium de Sanctis* is added at the top in a slightly later hand: De scō benedicto de Wermuth ℟ Os iusti Alleluia Justum deduxit. At the bottom in another xivth cent. hand: Tractus *Desiderium* non est in hoc libro (see fly-leaf).

S. Blasius is inserted in the margin before S. Agatha. We also find: SS. Vedastus and Amandus, Scholastica (Cedda B. C. and Oswin inserted) Cuthbert, Aelphege, (in the lower margin here is a late notary's device, the name R. Yond at the bottom, the initials I. A. C. round the top) Wilfrid, John of Beverley, Dunstan, (William of York inserted) Botulf, Alban, Ethedrida (*sic*), Karileph, Swithun, Boysil, Trans. of S. Thomas erased, Trans. of S. Swithun, Wandregesil, (S. Anne inserted, Transfiguration inserted) Osuuald, (Oswyn inserted), Magnus, Ebba, Aydan, Trans. of S. Cuthbert, (Thomas of Hereford inserted), Paulus (? Paulinus), Wilfrid, Romanus, Etheldrida, (Frydeswyda inserted, S. Edmund of Canterbury inserted), Edmund the King.

Four leaves from the end begins the *Tonarium*.

The book is evidently from Durham: but the *Catt. Vett.* do not admit of identifying it. The two fly-leaves at the end are also from service-books with music: the second has a hymn to S. Oswald.

23. Q. B. 6.

PSALTERIUM, ETC.

Vellum, $10\frac{5}{8} \times 7\frac{1}{2}$, ff. 141, varying numbers of lines to the page. Cent. xii and xv.

Binding: old boards with later back, formerly fastened with strap and pin. Given by Mr Man.

Collation: a^{12} (+ 12*) b^{14} (14 cancelled) c^{12}–g^{12} h^{10} (5–10 gone) i^{12} k^{8} (wants 8) || l^{8} m^{6} (4–6 canc.) || n^{4} || o $?^{12}$ (wants 2–5) p^{8} || q^{2} (wants 2).

Provenance: Durham. At the top of f. 15 is written in large letters of cent. xv.

Liber *dn̄i jo. cancellarii* ecclesie Cath. Dunelm. dn̄i... The words in italics seem to be written over something else; they have themselves been erased.

Contents:

1.	Ieronimus de camera Christi	f. 1
	Fundamentum ipsius camere est fides.	
2.	Origenes	1
	Psalterium est ita quasi magna domus.	
3.	Tables of days of the months and four seasons, etc. . .	1 *b*
4.	Kalendar	2
5.	Tables, Paschal Cycle, Table of the Moon	8
	In green, red, blue and black: a xvth century addition on p. 8 *a* and a xiiith cent. slip on f. 9 *b*.	
6.	Libellus b. Martini episcopi de quattuor uirtutibus . .	10
7.	Sermon. Sermo iste docet quales boni uel quales mali sint xpistiani. Oportet fratres karissimi ut tota mentis intentione	12 *b*
8.	Preliminary matter to the Psalter, in another hand, on thinner vellum.	
	Quot sint uirtutes psalmorum sanctus Augustinus dicit . .	14
	Canticum psalmorum animas decorat.	
	Orationes ante psalterium	14 *b*
9.	Psalterium, in double columns of 26 lines each . . .	15
	A collect follows each Psalm. The rubric to Ps. 1 is: Incipiunt tituli psalmorum: primus psalmus ostendit quod ipse erit lignum uite.	
	The seven nocturnes and *Quid gloriaris* have slightly larger initials, but not *Domine exaudi*.	
	Half a leaf is gone at *Dixit Dominus*, but the beginning of that Psalm remains.	
10.	Orationes post psalterium	84 *b*
11.	Cantica, ending with *Quicunque vult*	84 *b*
	The Litany has been cut out after f. 90.	
	Canticum in dominicis diebus	91
	Domine miserere nostri (Isa. xxxiii. 2–17).	
	Miserere domine plebi tue.	
	Cantica in aduentu domini	91 *b*
	Ecce dominus in fortitudine.	
	Cantate domino.	
	Hec dicit dominus.	

In natali domini 92
Populus qui ambulabat.
Letare ierusalem.
Vrbs fortitudinis.
Cantica in quadragesima . . . . 92 *b*
Deducant oculi mei.
Recordare domine.
Tollam quippe uos.
Cantica in resurrectione domini . . . . . . 93 *b*
Quis est iste.
Venite et reuertamur.
Expecta me.
Cantica de apostolis siue de martyribus 94
Vos sancti domini.
Fulgebunt iusti.
Reddet deus mercedem.
Cant. de uno martyre siue confessore 94
Beatus uir qui in sapientia.
Benedictus uir qui confidit.
Beatus uir qui inuentus.
Cant. de Virginibus . . . . 94 *b*
Audite me diuini.
Gaudens gaudebo.
Non uocaberis ultra.
In dedicatione ecclesie cantica 95
Letare ierusalem. Vrbs fortitudinis. Non uocaberis.
Hymni. Ad uesperas 95
O lux beata trinitas etc.
After the Hymn for the Purification is:
De S. Cuthberto ymnus 103
Magnus miles mirabilis.
Ad nocturnam:
Anglorum populi plaudite cuncti.
Ad laudes:
Adesto nobis inclite.
After Vincula S. Petri.
In natali S. Oswaldi R. et M. ymnus 105
Regalis ostro sanguinis.
Diuisio.
Christi fidelis armiger.

12. Office of the Dead in a hand of xvth century, 27 lines to a page 110

13. Collects and Antiphons, in another hand of cent. xv (?), in paler ink, double columns of 30 lines each 122

The first is for Pentecost. They include Collects for SS. Oswald (1), Thomas Becket, Blasius, Edmund of Canterbury, Leonard, Ebba, Cuthbert: after the Collect for Peace, they are almost all repeated, from the Collect for Pentecost to the Collect for Peace.

14. End of a Diurnal in the hand of cent. xii 126
Containing Antiphons, Collects, and Hymns for the Assumption, Pentecost, Michaelmas, S. Andrew, S. Oswald, S. Laurence and ymnus ad omnes horas de S. Maria.
Lux que luces in tenebris.
Prefulgens sol iusticie.
O christe proles uirginis.
Quem credimus ex uirgine.
Nate summe.
Fili marie.
O uirgo beatissima.

15. Sermo • Beati • Augustini • ypponiensis • Episcopi • de • dedicatione • ecclesie • . . . . 126 *b*
Quotiens cunque.
In the same hand: the title, in red capitals, is at the bottom of col. 1 of 126 *b*.

16. A Sermon without title on the same subject . . . . . 127 *b*
Recte festa ecclesie colunt.

17. De corpore uel sanguine domini uel quid significet quod hostia in tribus partibus diuiditur uel quid significent tres staciones que fiunt ante altare 128
Si contigerit pannum aliquem altaris.

18. Isydorus de homine erumpnas presentis seculi deflente . . 129
In subsequenti hoc libro qui nuncupatur sinonima.
On the verso of the leaf the form of writing changes from double columns to single lines, 36 to the page.
The last section is *De ypochrisi.*

19. De xv^cim^ signis . . . . 140 *b*
The usual passage, found by 'Ieronimus in annalibus hebreorum.'

20. A Table of Easter, on a smaller leaf of cent. xv 141
Easter is calculated for the years 1383–1443.

The most interesting portion of the book is perhaps the Kalendar; it is beautifully written, the green and blue inks being of especially fine colour. There are several insertions of cent. xv.

Feb. S. Blasius *inserted.*
Mar. S. Cedda *inserted.*
S. Oswin Reg. M. *inserted.*
Cuthbert in red, *Capp.*
Ap. S. Guthlac.
Aelphege.
May. S. Iohannes archiep. in beuerl.
Dunstan.
S. Godrici heremite de Finchal *inserted.*
Commemoracio bede presbiteri. Capp. xii. lect. *inserted.*
June 5. Obitus Iohannis...... *inserted xv cent. and erased.*
S. William Ep. Ebor. *inserted cent. xiii in small hand.*

	Botulf.
	Alban.
	Ætheldritha.
June 30.	Marcialis *inserted cent. xiii.*
July 1.	Carilephus abb.
7.	S. Boisil presb.
	Wandregisil abb.
	S. Anne xii. lect. *inserted cent. xv.*
Aug.	S. Osuualdus in green and his octave in black.
20.	S. Oswyn *inserted cent. xv.*
25.	S. Ebba *inserted cent. xiii.*
31.	S. Aidan in red, S. Aenspiþe.
Sept.	Trans. S. Cuthbert in blue and octave in red.
Oct.	Paulinus.
	Wilfrid.
	Aetheldritha.
	Romanus archiep. in green.
Nov.	Deposicio Edmundi Cant. *inserted cent. xv.*
	Eadmundi K. M.

There is a good initial to Beatus uir (f. 15) in green and red, interlaced, with two leopards (?) and a man.

24. Q. B. 7.

TRACTATUS THEOLOGICI.

Vellum, $10\frac{1}{2} \times 7\frac{5}{8}$, ff. 143, mostly in double columns of 42 lines each. Cent. xiv.

Binding: wooden boards rebacked: formerly fastened with two clasps. Given by Mr Man.

Collation: a^4 b^8 c^{12} d^{12} e^{14} f^{12} (11, 12 cancelled) g^{12} (+ 2 leaves inserted between 10 and 11) h^{12}–k^{12} l^{14} m^{16} n^4 (4 cancelled).

The book is most likely from Durham, to which the Kalendar (no. 10) belongs: on the last page is the name John Richardson.

The 2nd leaf of the text begins (*mar*)*moribus diuersi coloris.*

Contents:

On f. 2 *b* is an old table of contents (cent. xv) as follows:

In hoc libro subscripto sunt contenta

1. In primis Quidam tractatus de morte et eius circumstanciis . f. 1
   Inc. Quia ad mortem tendimus omnes.
2. Item Sermo de S. Benedicto 9
   Festiua beatissimi Benedicti solempnitas.

3. Item speculum religiosorum 13
Accipite uos religiosi hoc speculum.

4. Item Expositio de sex alis Cherub 51
With a diagram of the Cherub, in black and red.
This is in another somewhat earlier hand.
Item Explanacio turris sapiencie . . . . 54 *b*
This entry is erased. It is apparently another name for no. 5.

5. Item speculum theologie factum a magistro Johanne Welensi . 55
A diagram of the tower of wisdom, followed by trees of virtues and vices.

6. Item Explanacio ligni uite 58
Referring to the previous diagrams.
ff. 58 *b*–60 *b* are blank.

7. Item Vita Aluredi Abbatis Rievall. (per W. Daniel) . . 61
Patri et domino eximie sanctitatis viro Mauricio suo Walterus Danielis.
Item Lamentacio auctoris vite eiusdem de eadem re . . 74
In exordio in processu et in fine lamentacionis mee ne ridiculus appaream.

8. Item Aluredus Abbas Rieuallen. de oneribus sed incomplete . 75 *b*
To G. Bishop of London.
Dilecto et diligendo et cum omni deuocionis dulcedine amplectendo sancto patri G. Londoniensi episcopo.
The index (f. 79) gives 31 homilies: the text ends in the xviith.
Proiciuntur autem (?) quasi stirpis inutilis cui nihil aliud debetur quam ignis. Dicit etiam *ipse* (catchword).

9. Item Notule de historia aurea collectae 111
Excerpciones quedam breues siue notule ex historia aurea omnium historiarum matre collecte.
From the Creation to A.D. 1347.
f. 124 *b* is blank.

10. Item Kalendarium plenum nominibus sanctorum quolibet die per annum 125
An abbreviated Martyrology: the names of the places where the Saints suffered etc., are written above their names. Each day occupies one line; e.g. Jan. 1:

	rome	uia appia	rome	spoleto
Circumcisio.	Almachii mart.	30 militum.	Martine V.	Concordii P. M.

cesarea capadocie	affrica ruspensi ecclesia	lugdun. territorio	Allexandrie
Basilii Ep.	Fulgencii Ep.	Augendi Abb.	Eufrosine V.

In red are Depositio Cuthberti and Oswald.

11. Item legenda de Sancta Elizabeth 131
Quoniam, ut legitur in Eccl. 43 gloria domini plenum est opus eius.

12. Item Meditaciones S. Augustini . . . . 136 *b*
Vigili cura mente solicita summo conatu.

25. Q. B. 8.

TRACTATUS DE ASTRONOMIA, ETC.

Vellum, 10 × 7½, ff. 111, varying numbers of lines to a page, two volumes in one. Cent. xii.

Binding: two sheets of a Psalter of cent. xiii, in double columns of 27 lines each, containing parts of Psalms ix. and xvii.–xxiv. (Lat.).

Given by Mr Man.

Collation: a^{10} b^{8} || a^{8}–l^{8} m^{8} (6, 7 cancelled, 8 attached to cover).

Provenance: almost certainly Durham. On f. 1 *a* a mark has been erased, but the press-mark A. occurs twice, and also A. 22. The entries are three:

(1) a. Sermones S. Augustini.
(2) a. Sermones diuersi cum tractatu de planetis.
(3) a. Tractatus de temporibus sole luna stellis ventis terra mari et aliis similibus.
2. 2. Sermones quidam S. Augustini et quidam Jeronimi.

The 2nd leaf of the text begins

dies prosperitatem seculi significat.

It is the book in *Catt. Vett.* 75, A. Sermones diuersi cum tractatu de planetis, ii fo., "serit et cum."

Contents:

I. An anonymous Tract on the day and night stars, etc., with special reference to the Bible: in an early xiith century hand: 40 lines to a page . . . . f. 1

The source seems to be Isidore, *de naturis rerum* 38, 44, etc.

It begins without title or space for a first initial at the top of f. 1 *b*.

Aegiptii autem ex initio noctis sequentis diei originem tradunt; romani medio noctis oriri diem uolunt: et in medium noctis finiri.

In the rest of the tract spaces are left for initials and diagrams, none of which are filled in.

The contents are as follow:

§ 1, of which the opening lines have been given, ends on f. 2 *a*:
Equinoxiales dies s(unt) in quibus dies et nox equalibus horarum spatiis euoluuntur.

§ 2. (N)ox est solis absentia . . . . f. 2

3. (E)BDOMADA apud grecos et romanos.
On f. 2 *b* is a space for a diagram.

4. (M)ENSIS EST luminis lunaris circuitus . . . . . . 2 *b*
This sentence occurs on f. 3.
Plerique autem asserunt cignum sabinorum regem prius annum in menses diuisisse.
5. (S)ic ambrosius: tempora sunt uices mutationum . . . 3 *b*
6. (D)uorum temporum hec sunt principia 4
Space for a diagram.
7. (S)olsticia duo sunt . . . . 4 *b*
8. (M)vndvs est uniuersitas.
8. Ceterum sanctus ambrosius eadem elimenta 5
9. (C)elum spiritualiter ecclesia.
Space for a diagram.
10. (A)mbrosius sanctus in libro exameron sic loquitur . . 6
11. (H)ec est ambrosii sententia. Aquas super celos.
12. (H)ec sunt uerba ambrosii in libro exameron.
13. (R)ursus in eodem opere doctor idem . . . . . . 6 *b*
14. (D)icunt antiqui aratus et eginus solem per semet ipsum moueri.
15. (S)anctus Augustinus in psalmi decimi expositione . . . 7 *b*
Rough diagram in the margin and several sketches in the text of the moon.
16. (L)unam quidem per hos ortus et occasus ait eginus . . 8
17. (S)olem sapientes dicunt altius currere . . . . . . 8 *b*
18. (N)on deficit luna sed obumbratur . . . . 8 *b*
19. (S)telle quidem cum mundo uertuntur 9
20. (I)n ambitu quippe celestium orbium.
21. (S)telle non habere proprium lumen . . . . . . 9 *b*
Space for a diagram.
22. (F)alsa autem et uulgaris opinio est nocte stellas cadere . . 10
23. (L)egitur in iob.
24. (A)rcturus est ille quem latini septentrionem dicunt . . 10 *b*
25. (A)mbrosium in libro exameron legi dicentem . . . 11 *b*
26. (T)onitrua autem ex fragore nubium 12
27. (D)icunt naturalium scriptores causarum.
28. (C)lemens Romanus antistes et martir ita scripsit:
Arcus enim in aere ex imagine solis . . . . . . 12 *b*
29. (N)otandum ex libro iob 13
30. (L)egitur in amos propheta qui uocat aquas maris.
31. (A)it ambrosius quod plerumque glacialibus uentorum . . 13 *b*
32. (S)imili quoque ratione grandinum.
33. (V)entus est commotus et agitatus aer 14
34. (P)rimus cardinalis septentrion.
35. Quosdam tranquillus proprios locorum flatus certis appellat uocabulis . . . . 14 *b*
Space for a diagram.
36. (T)empestas turbo est.
37. (P)estilentia morbus late uagans . . . . 15 *b*
38. (C)ur oceanus reciprocis estibus revertitur.
Lucan is quoted.

39. (C)ur mare maius non fiat...clemens episcopus ait: Non crescit mare eo quod naturaliter salsa aqua 16
40. (R)ursus idem ambrosius doctor docuit dicens: Mare iccirco dicunt 16 *b*
41. (E)giptus aeris calorem per solem habet.
42. (I)n pratis tranquillus sic asserit dicens: Extremum mare oceanus est.
43. (Q)ualiter terra super aerem fundata 17
44. (S)apientes dicunt terram in modum spongie esse conceptam . 17 *b*
Vnde et salustius uentis inquit per caua terre precipitatis rupti sunt aliquot montes tumulique.
45. (D)e monte autem ethna Iustinus in libro historiarum ita scripsit dicens: Sicilie insule tellus tenuis ac fragilis est.
Ends (f. 18 *a*): Sic ignis ille gehenne ad comburenda corpora damnatorum finem nunquam habiturus est.

II. Sermones S. Augustini 19

A xvth century title at the top reads:

a. Sermones diuersi Aug.

They are in a beautiful xiith century hand, in double columns of 41 lines each. The majority have no titles.

1. De episcopis et unitate ecclesie.
Dicit apostolus paulus. Non est potestas nisi a deo.
3. Sermo in dedicacione ecclesie.
Salomon edificauit domum.
7. De Sacerdotibus.
Labia sacerdotis custodiunt scientiam.
8. De Sacerdotibus.
Locutus est dominus ad moysen.
9. De Sacerdotibus.
Qui descendunt mare in maribus.
10. Alius sermo de Sacerdotibus.
Deus stetit in synagoga deorum.
11. De ciuitate dei.
Fundamenta eius.
12. Sermo. In quo pater conqueritur De vinea sua per similitudinem
Si quis diligit me.
13. Sermo De carne contra spiritum et de ·v· sensibus corporis.
Scitote fratres karissimi quia uetus homo.
14. Sermo de aduentu summi iudicis et quomodo Adam non seruauit preceptum domini.
15. Sermo ad populum in quadragesima.
16. Sermo in quo docetur quid sit agendum in ecclesia.
17. Alius sermo de sacerdotibus.
Locutus—moysen dicens: homo de semine Aaron.
18. Sermo de adventu domini.
Consolamini.
19. Sermo de dedicatione.
Facta sunt encenia.

20. de contemplatiuis.
21. de significatione crucis.
22. de rogationibus.
23. de pentecosten.
    Uerbo domini celi firmati sunt.
24. de sacerdotibus.
    Homo quidam peregre.
25. de eodem.
    designauit dominus.
26. de leproso et paralithico in Dom. 1 post Theophaniam.
27. de pigris hominibus in peccatis morantibus.
29. In xlma.
    Factum est uerbum domini ad ieremyam dicens: quid tu uides.
32. de perseueratione.
33. de vanitate secularium cogitationum.
34. in xlma.
    Maria soror moysi peccauit.
35. in purificat. S. Marie.
36. de sanctimonialibus.
37. de aduentu domini.
    Dicite filie syon.
38. de pentecosten.
    Dum complerentur dies.
39. ad fideles qui sunt pugnaturi contra mundum.
41. in rogationibus.
    Confitemini alterutrum.
42. de ascensione domini.
43. de resurrect. domini.
44. de cena domini.
45. de presbiteris.
    Factum est uerb. dom. ad Ezechielem.
46. de eodem.
    Posuit moyses labrum.
47. in xlma.
    Noli emulari.
48. de eodem.
    Ecce odor fili mei.

After no. 60.

61. Psalterium rome positum positus emendaui (Jerome, to Paula and Eustochium).
62. On the x commandments and x plagues.
92. is on the death of S. John Evangelist.

Profert enim historia quod cum esset Iohannes nonaginta et vii annorum apparuit ei dominus.

There are 96 in all.

26. Q. B. 9.

EGIDIUS ROMANUS DE REGIMINE PRINCIPUM.

Vellum, $9\frac{3}{4} \times 6\frac{3}{4}$, ff. 262, in double columns of 32 lines each. Cent. xv.

Written in England, in a fine upright hand. Bound in old stamped leather over boards: the clasps are gone. There is an old press-mark: *Classis 2dae dextrae lib:* 51. The number 51 is also stamped on the edge of the leaves.

On the fly-leaf is:

17° Decembris 1633.

Franc: Hughes vnus ex Armigeris Bedellis amicissimus vir et benefactor dono dedit amoris ergo.

Collation: a^{10} (1 blank, 9 cancelled) b^8–ii^8 kk^6 (3 cancelled, 6 blank).

F. 1 *a* has a border of French-Flemish work, the style of which is later than that of the rest of the ornamental work. It is divided into triangles with grounds of fluid gold, blue and red, with flowers and flourishes. There is also a miniature, occupying three-fourths of the text-space, of the Descent of the Holy Ghost: the Virgin and 17 others are kneeling in a room: above are the Father and Son throned, probably sending down the Dove. This part of the painting has been partly erased. The style of it is very bad. In the lower margin are these arms. Quarterly *azure* and *gules*, four lions *or* rampant gardant. On a chief *argent* wavy, 3 besants *sable.* Throughout the book, at the *L.* of each column, is a kind of ornament topped with a fleur-de-lys alternately gold and blue, and with demi fleurs-de-lys, alternately gold and blue, springing out of it all the way up.

There are a certain number of marginal notes.

27. Q. B. 10.

SS. AMBROSII ET HIERONYMI QUAEDAM.

Vellum, $10\frac{1}{8} \times 6\frac{3}{8}$, ff. 144, 33 lines to a page. Cent. xii.

Written in England probably. Binding, white skin over boards flat back: formerly fastened with strap and pin.

On f. 4 *b* is:

Lib. Magistri Andree Doket
rectoris Sancti Botulfi Cantabr.

He was first Master of Queens' College (1448–1484).

Collation: i^4 (fly-leaves) a^8 (1 cancelled) b^8–f^8 g^8 (wants 5) h^8 i^8 k^8 (wants 1) l^8–o^8 p^{10} q^8 r^6 s^8 (7 cancelled).

Contents:

1. Libellus ualde utilium preceptorum atque consiliorum de libris officiorum Beatissimi pape (erased) Ambrosii mediolanensis collectus . . . . f. 5

The title is in red and green: and there is a large red and green initial.

Inc. Non arrogans uideri arbitror si inter filios.

There are rubricated headings to the extracts.

On f. 50 *b*.

Explicit defloratio librorum beati Ambrosii de officiis.

Incipiunt capitulationes sequentis libri.

The capitula of the two books of the next treatise follow.

2. Liber S. Jeronimi presbyteri contra Iouinianum 52

In a different but not later hand.

The second book begins on f. 87 *b*.

3. Liber beati Ambrosii Mediolanensis episcopi de misteriis siue iniciandis . . . . 117 *b*

There is a remarkable initial of white interlaced work, enclosing spaces of red, green, and purple: a dragon at the top.

4. Sermo primus de sacramentis ambrosii 125

The hand is the same: the initial very plain and rough, red and green.

Inc. De sacramentis que accepistis sermonem adorior.

Sermo ii.
In diluuio quoque figuram baptismatis 128

Sermo iii.
Hesterno de fonte 131

Sermo iv.
In ueteri testamento 133

Sermo v.
Hesterno sermo noster 136

Sermo vi.
Sicut uerus deus est . . . . 139 *b*

Sermo vii.
Magnitudo celestium beneficiorum . . . . . . 142 *b*

On f. 143 *b* the hand becomes suddenly much smaller.

On f. 144 *b*, in a xvth cent. hand, is:

Walterus at the noke R. non habuit Johannem.

On the fly-leaves at the beginning are the following matters:

(1) Two beginnings of a dedicatory Epistle

Diu me reluctantem, pater serenissime,
Multum diuque me reluctantem, pater syncerissime.

There are inside the cover and on f. 1 *a*:

(2) Three extracts from Gregorius super Ezechielem . . . f. 1 *b*
(3) Original (xiith cent.) table to the extracts from Ambrose . 2 *a*
(4) A list of herbs, mostly in English (xvth cent.), arranged in four *cedule.*

Inc. *Prima cedula.*
Elena campana.
ffenel reed.
Radycoll and radych.
Solsarium.
Tansey.
Wernothe.

Followed by a long receipt in English, beginning:

Ffyrste sede ye herbis as yey be wrytyne in lyk porcion & yen putt theym in a gret vessel & whassh them . . . . . . 2 *b*, 3 *a*

28. Q. B. 11.

PRISCIANUS.

Vellum, $10\frac{1}{4} \times 6\frac{3}{8}$, ff. 129, 41 lines to a page. Cent. xi.
Given by Mr Man.

Collation: a^8 (1 and 8 loose)–c^8 d^{10} e^8–g^8 h^8 (8 cancelled) i^8–l^8 m^8 (7, 8 gone, replaced by 2 leaves of cent. xiii, xiv) n^8 (1 gone, replaced by 1 leaf of cent. xiii, xiv) o^8 p^8 q^8: quires numbered later i–xvi on lower margin of last page of each.

The book comes from Durham. On f. 1 *b* is the letter N, and on what should be f. 2 *a* (now 3 *a*) is

Pricianus in maiori et de accentibus de communi libraria monachorum dunelm.

In the Catalogue of the "Spendemente" (1391, *Catal. Vett.* p. 49) is the entry:

N. Liber Prisciani in magno. ii fo., "bile est aliquid,"

which answers to this copy.

Possibly it may be one of two Priscians left by Bp Hugo Pudsey in 1195 (l. c. 118).

The contents are:

1. The Greek alphabet and numerals . . . . f. 1 *a*
   Some nearly illegible matter in Latin . . . . . . 1 *a*
2. Prisciani de Grammatica Libri xvi . . . . 1 *b*
3. Priscianus de Accentibus 129

Ending imperfectly:

si penultimam correptam habent ante penultimam.

The ornaments of the book, such as they are, are interesting. The initial to the whole work (f. 1 *b*) is of white and blue on a red ground, and contains a picture in outline of Priscian in a pointed cap and embroidered dress, writing at a desk, on a scroll inscribed:

Sum romanorum corrector grammaticorum.

The initial to book viii is better drawn and better preserved: the colours used are the same. In it a boy in tunic and blue shoes is climbing among the interlacements. The tract *de accentibus* has a very Celtic initial, with plaited work.

It may be of interest to add some notice of the Greek alphabet and numerals which appear on f. 1 *a*. They are arranged in this form:

i	ii	iii	iiii	v	vi	vii	viii
una (for mia)	diω	tris	tessaris	pente	hexa	hepta	ogda
alpha	beta	gamma	delta	e b*re*uis	episima	zeta	eta
A	B	Γ	λ	Є	S	Z	H

ix	x	xv	xxx	xl	l	lx	lxx
ennea	...(? deca)	pimoicosi	trienta	saranta	pentinta	hexinta	hecdointa
teta	iota	cappa	lapda	mi	ni	xi	o b*re*uis
Θ	I	K	ʎ	)-(	)-	Ξ	O

lxxx	lxxxx	c	cc	ccc	cccc	d
ogdoinda	kopeneinta	ecaton	diacos	triacos	tetracos	pentacos
pi	copi	ro	sigma	tau	i	fi
Π	y	P	C	Ꞇ	Y	Φ

dc	dcc	dccc	dcccc
exacos	heptacos	octacos	kcennecos
chi	psi	octomega	ennaches
X	Ψ	ω	ϡ

The almost illegible lower half of the page is, partly at least, in French (cent. xiii, early). In the first line (about the middle) I can read:

estre eledh chiet. Seint acharie la pn̄t ......en sun la. os ais nerf.

The last part is in Latin: the last line but one begins, et pedes crucifixi.

The whole, French and Latin, fills 20 lines.

29. Q. B. 12.

Extracts from the Constitutions of Clement V.

Vellum, $9\frac{3}{4} \times 6$, ff. 64, 25 lines to a page. Cent. xv (early).

Binding: modern leather over old boards: formerly fastened with strap and pin. Given by Mr Man.

Fly-leaf from a MS. of xiiith cent. in double columns (Canon Law).

Collation: a^8–c^8 d^6 e^8–g^8 h^{10}.

Provenance. Durham. At the top of f. 1 are the remains of two inscriptions, the greater part of which has been torn off: of the first only the word *liber* remains. Of the second

h. Textus septimi . . . . h. .

It was no doubt written at Durham College, Oxford (see the Colophon), and sent to Durham at a later period: the second of the two inscriptions is certainly a Durham one. The book does not occur in the *Catt. Vett.*

Colophon, in red:

Nomen scriptoris est thomas plenus amoris
Iste liber constat Petro de Abẏngdun.
Stephano

The line about the writer's name (often supposed to stand for Fullalove) is common in Oxford MSS. e.g. *Univ.* cod. cxlii.

Contents:

1. Iohannes xxij^{us} dilectis filiis doctoribus et scolaribus vniuersis Oxonie commorantibus salutem et apostolicam benedictionem.

De summa trinitate et fide catholica ℞. Clemens v^{us}.

Fidei catholice fundamento......

ends: Clemens quintus in generali constitucione vienn.

2. De rescript. ℞.

Abbates aut alii religiosi.

A good many leaves are palimpsest: the earlier writing is in double columns, very small, of cent. xiii or xiv.

30. Q. B. 13.

MIRACULA B. V. MARIE.
WYCLIFFE'S GOSPELS.

Vellum, 9 × 6, ff. 50, varying numbers of lines to a page, two volumes in one. Cent. xiv, xv.

Given by Mr Man.

Collation: a? (wants 2, ...: last cancelled) b⁴ c¹² (wants 8) || a⁸ b¹⁰ (7 cancelled) c⁸ d⁸.

Contents:

I. 1. A fragment imperfect at both ends, cent. xiv . . . . f. 1

The first leaf is half the breadth of the rest: and the number of lines is 38. It begins abruptly

succenditur et ei sublimior efficitur. Tali nimirum solitudo congeritur qui consortem.

The verso ends:

pro seipso non pro suis amans et se totum in amato figens.

2. xii capituli, imperfect 2

Inc. ...bilibus leticiis possidetur. Immo non est meritum hominis.

Expl. cum ineffabili iubilacione et melodia ipsum eternaliter laudare cui sit honor et gloria in secula seculorum. Amen.

Expliciunt xii capituli, etc.

3. Bernardus de dignitate clericorum . . . . 2 *b*

O quantam dignitatem contulit vobis deus.

4. De uita b. M. virginis . . . . 3 *b*

Circa uirginem uero ex qua incarnacio facta fuit.

...rediit in nazareth que qualiter fuit facta inuenies in legenda de natiuitate sua. Expl. vita b. Marie. Scriptoris miseri dignare deus miserere . . . . 4 *b*

5. Incipiunt quedam miracula de S. Maria . . . . . . 4 *b*

In another hand of cent. xv, and paler ink.

The miracles are:

1. De latrone a suspensione liberato (the thief Ebbo).
   Sicut exponit b. Gregorius de vij stellis.
2. De clerico extra cimiterium sepulto.
   Quidam clericus erat in vrbe castonensi.
3. Quo modo pro gaudio quinquies predicato gaudium promittitur.
   ...lier quoque quidam clericus.
4. De duabus mulieribus.
   Coniux cuiusdam cum maximo odio pelici.

5. De duabus ymaginibus.
Sunt in constantinopoli due ymagines.

6. De clerico ab episcopo ut filius amato. (In verse.)
Huc venite et audite omnes serui domini.

7. De monacho de ewglesham (Evesham).
Illud quoque non omittendum de egueshamensi monacho.

These are all common stories: many copies of them are described in the British Museum *Catalogue of Romances*, vol. ii.

6. Hic incipiunt meditaciones de passione. Et primo ponitur meditacio de cena domini. Secundo de passione in generali etc. ut infra patet 8

In a hand of early xvth cent., 42 lines to a page.

Inc. Adueniente iam et imminente tempore miseracionum.

The meditation de passione (f. 10) begins:

Occurrit nunc ut de passione domini nostri Ihesu tractemus.

It is divided into sections for the Seven Hours: the meditation for Vespers is imperfect at the beginning.

On f. 17 *b* (the last of this portion of the volume) is:

Thys ys Iohn̄ medylton bok. (Cent. xv.)

II. The Gospels of SS. Matthew, Mark and Luke in English.

In a very small hand of cent. xv (early). The first three leaves of the text of S. Matthew are very beautifully written: after that the writing is smaller and more pointed, and the ink paler: 53 lines to a page.

On f. 1 *a* is only a note (cent. xv):

Nota textus in sacra pagina contra simulacra Exod. 20mo c^{o} $Leuitic^{o}$ 7mo c^{o} leuitic. 26mo c^{o} etc.

The last text is:

20 $parali^{mon}$ 14mo c^{o}.

On f. 1 *b*:

Heer bigynneþ a prologe on matheu
Matheu $þ^{t}$ was of iudee.

On f. 2 *a* the text begins: (T)he book of generacion of Ihū Criste.

S. Luke's Gospel is imperfect: ending in ix. 24:

for he þat wele make his liif saaf shal leese it & he.

31. Q. B. 14.

BEDAE MARTYROLOGIUM.

Vellum, 9 × 6½, ff. 43, 31 lines to a page. Cent. xiii.

Vellum binding over pasteboards. Given by Mr Man.

Collation: a^{8}–d^{8} e^{10} (4, 5, 8–10 cancelled) || f^{6} (1 being the first fly-leaf).

Part of a Papal bull or other document of cent. xv is pasted into the cover. Some Kalendar notes of cent. xv are inside the cover and on the fly-leaf.

A quire is lost after *b*, containing from iii Id. Mai to xix Kal. Aug. inclusive. Quire *c* is in a somewhat larger hand. There are a good many notes added in cent. xiv, xv, e.g.:

iii Kal. Jan. In prouincia Merciorum apud Euesham Sc̄i E(g)wini Ep. et Conf.
vi Id. Jan. Depositio S. Wlstini Ep. Conf.
v ,, In Brittannia ciuitate Cantuarie monasterio S. Petri Ap. beati Adriani Abbatis.
Id. Jan. In Scotia ciuitate Glascuensi S. Kentigerni.
xiv Kal. Feb. Nat. S. Branwaladri Ep.
xiii ,, In Scocia S. Vigiani Conf.
iii Non. Feb. In ciuitate doribornia S. Laurencii Archiep. et Conf.
ii ,, Dep. S. Edburge V. Eodem die S. Gilberti conf.
Id. Feb. S. Ermenilde V.
xiii Kal. Mar. S. Winwaloi doctoris.

There are many similar mentions of English and foreign saints, and references to Bede's History. On xviii Kal. Nov. we have, Et dedicacio ecclesie de Bathewyk: and on xiv Kal. Nov., Eboraci memoria reliquiarum ecclesie S. Petri.

viii Kal. Nov. Transl. S. Johannis Ebor. Archiep.
ii Id. Dec. In hiberniâ S. Ffinani Conf.
Id. Dec. S. Judoci. In Cancia apud La . bias S. Eadburge V.

The martyrology is followed by

1. A Form of cursing sacrilegious persons.
2. A statement of what a parish priest ought to know and to do.
3. Later verses on the months.
4. The hymn *Saluatoris mater pia*, with music on a 4-line stave.
5. In a later hand. Eight sets, each of three lessons, *de beata Maria*.

32. Q. B. 15.

TRACTATUS CONTRA VITIA, ETC.

Paper, $9\frac{3}{8} \times 7$, ff. 102. Cent. xv (late).

Binding: leather over original boards: clasp gone. This is no. 7 in James's list, *Eclog. Cant.* p. 137.

Collation: a^{10} b^{10} c^{12} || d^{12}–h^{12} i^{12} (11, 12 gone).

Contents:

1. Quadripartitus apologeticus b. Cyrilli Episc. . . . . . f. 1
   In double columns of 43 lines. Book i is gone.
   Incipit primum cap. secundi libri. De bono humilitatis et malo superbie. Vmefactus aer.
   f. 10. Exp. lib. secundus de hijs que sunt contra superbiam.
   Inc. lib. tercius de hijs que sunt contra auariciam.
   f. 20 *b*. Lib. iv. De hijs que sunt contra luxuriam.
   f. 24 *b*. *Expl.* quadripartitus apologeticus Beati Cyrilli Ep. In quo quidem speculum limpidissimum omnis sapiencie claret.
2. Libellus de iv uirtutibus 25
   Quatuor uirtutum species.
   30 lines to a page: with comment.
3. Tract. de doctrina dicendi atque tacendi 28 (29)
   Si fore uis sapiens.
4. Diagrams of two hands, with a subject of meditation inscribed on each joint or part. On one is:

   Dat manus hec doctis que sit meditacio noctis,

   on the other:

   Hec manus ex rebus iubet hiis tractare diebus.

   f. 30 *b*, 31 *a* (31, 32)
5. Epistolae Senece ad Lucilium numero lxxxv. 32 (33)
   29 lines to a page: in another hand.
   Ending in Ep. lxxxiv.

   vestibula, non in prerupto tantum istic (stabis).

   The last words are supplied in a hand of cent. xvii.

33. Q. B. 16.

P. VERGILII MARONIS AENEIS.

Vellum, $9\frac{1}{8} \times 4\frac{3}{4}$, ff. 103, 49 lines to a page. Cent. xii, xv.

'E dono Thomae Wood.' It is no. 6 in James's *Ecloga Cantabrigiensis*, p. 137.

Binding: original boards covered with leather of cent. xvii, xviii.

Collation: blank fly-leaf: a^8 (4 and 5 supply) wants 1, 2: b^8–k^8 l^8 (8 cancelled and supplied: cent. xv) m^8 (supply, cent. xv) n^{10} (cent. xv: 10 gone: blank).

The hand is good: it appears to change in quire g and to become larger. The original copy seems to have been made from an imperfect archetype: f. 1 *a* is blank: the text begins imperfectly: f. 93 *b* was originally blank. This page and ff. 94–103 (as well as ff. 3, 4) are written in a late xvth cent. hand.

The initials of the books are plain green or red.

There are marginal and interlinear glosses in at least four hands: 1, contemporary; 2, of cent. xiii, xiv; 3, of cent. xv, by the scribe who supplied the latter leaves; 4, of cent. xv, xvi, resembling an Italian hand.

The text begins at *Aen.* i. 230.

Eternis regis imperiis et fulmine terres.

The two supply leaves contain the lines

l. 277. Moenia Romanosque suo de nomine dicet

to

466. Namque uidebat uti bellantes Pergama circum.

The xvth century hand supplies all after

xii. 108. Aeneas acuit hastam et se suscitat ira.

Books vii–xii have the arguments in hexameters.

The shape of the book indicates that it was intended, not for the shelf, but for the wallet. The number 14 is branded on the edges.

34. Q. B. 17.

TRACTATUS MISCELLANEI.

Vellum, $8\frac{1}{2} \times 6$, ff. 137, varying numbers of lines to a page. Cent. xii, xiii.

Given by Mr Man.

Binding: modern leather over old boards: has had either clasp or strap and pin.

Provenance. Rievaulx: on f. 7 *b* is Liber sc̄e Marie Rieuall: on 47 *b* Lib. S. M. Rieuallis: and again on f. 109 *a*.

Collation: a^6 || b^8 || c^8 d^8 (see post) e^8 f^8 (wants 8) || g^2 h^8 i^8 (wants 8) || k^8 l^8 m^{10} (wants 10) n^6 o^6 || p^8 (+ 8* -da sunt) || q^8 || r^2 (wants 2) s^8 t^8 (wants 8) || u^6 (wants 6).

The plan of quire d is as follows:

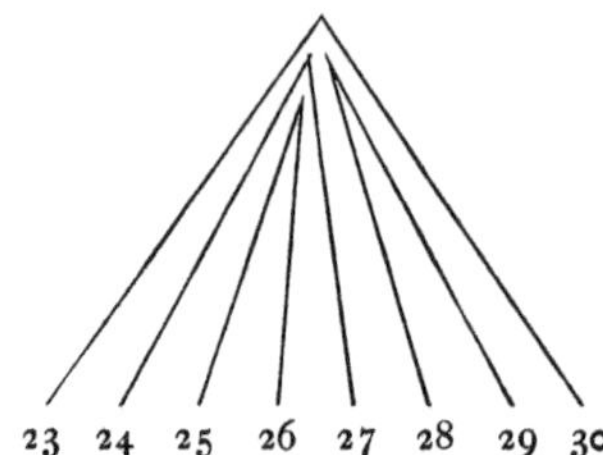

Contents:

1. Catalogue of the books in the Library at Rievaulx. Cent. xiii. . 1 *a*
2. Introductiones in Theologiam . . . . 7 *a*
   Introducendis in facultatem theologicam quedam compendiose prelibanda sunt.
   In 2 columns of 38 lines each. Cent. xiii.
3. Fallacie. Fallacia apud logicos dicitur . . . . . 9 *b*
   Same hand.
4. Loci. Locus argumenti est sedes argumenti . . . . . 12 *b*
   Same hand.
   14 *b* is blank.
5. Summa de diuersa uocabulorum significacione edita a mag. Will. de monte. Called at the end, Tropi theologici (43 *b*) followed by a few miscellaneous extracts . . . . . 15 *a*
   In two columns of 38 lines. Cent. xiii.
   f. 46 *b* is blank.
6. Notes on vices. Cent. xiii. 46
   f. 47 is blank.
7. Exempla moralia. Ad edificacionem animarum et morum informacionem. Cent. xiii. 2 cols. 38 lines . . . . 48 *a*
8. Sermons without heading in a fine hand of cent. xiii, 34 lines to the page . . . . 63 *a*
   1. Hora est iam uos de sompno surgere. More boni sacriste.
   2. .... Excitare uolens apostolus.
   3. Deus manifeste ueniet deus noster non silebit. Uerba Dauid.
9. Aelredi Abbatis Rieuallensis oracio pastoralis . . . . 97 *a*
   O bone pastor Jhesu. Cent. xiii. 34 lines to a page.
   On 99 *a* are two extracts of cent. xv; one from Ep. xxi. of Aelred; the other his dying words.
   99 *b* is blank.
10. Consuetudines Cisterciensium . . . . 100 *a*
    Cent xii, xiii: in a beautiful hand: double columns of 31 lines each: ends with the Priuilegium Innocencii pape in a different hand . . . . 107 *a*

11. Stephanus cisterciensis ecclesie seruus to T. Abbot of scireburne . . . . 108 *b*

12. Bernardi Antiphonarium siue liber de Musica . . . . 109 *a*
Cent. xii, xiii, 30 lines to a page.
Tonale in smaller writing . . . . 116 *a*
Quid est tonale. Magister. Regula naturam et formam cantuu*m* regularium determinans.
117 *a* is blank. 117 *b* has memorial verses on the number of chapters in each book of the Bible.

13. Bernardi siluestris liber de creatione rerum . . . . . 118 *a*
Cent. xiii: well written, 39 lines to a page.
Dedicated to Terricus. Interspersed with verses after the manner of Boethius and Martianus Capella.
133 *a* is blank.

14. Lines on prosody with interlinear notes.
Regula splendescit quia sillaba longa patescit . . . . 133 *b*
Sincopa de medio tollit quod epentesis auget.
Aufert appocope finem quem dat paragoge.
Cent. xii, xiii, 34 lines to a page.
137 is blank, with scribbles of cent. xvi.

I append a copy of the Catalogue which occupies ff. 1–6, though it has been already printed in Wright and Halliwell's *Reliquiae Antiquae*, II. pp. 180–189, and also in Edward Edward's *Memoirs of Libraries*, I. p. 333–341.

It is perhaps worth remarking that the comparatively small amount of secular literature which the list contains was probably a common feature in Cistercian Libraries, at least in the early days of the order.

f. 1 *a*

(rubr.) Hi sunt libri *sancte* marie Rieuall*ensis*.

A

line erased.
odex iustiniani.
ecreta graciani.
ohannes super decreta.
aẏmo super epistolas pauli.

B

Augustinus de ciuitate dei in uno volumine.
" super Johannem in uno volumine.
" super psalterium in quinque voluminibus.
" de decem preceptis de gratia et libero arbitrio et epistola prosperi ad Aug. et epistola hylarii ad Aug. et Aug. de predestinatione sanctorum. de bono perseverantie et Aug. super genesim contra manicheos in 1°. vol.
Aug. de sermone domini in monte. et de natura et gratia et epistola eiusdem ad ualentinum in .1°. uol.
Aug. de quantitate anime. et Ambrosius de bono mortis et de fuga seculi. et de viduis in .1°. uol.
Aug. de perfeccione iusticie. de correptione et gratia. et dominus uobiscum in .1°. uol.
Aug. de caritatȩ. et retractationes eiusdem in uno voluminȩ.

Aug. de duabus animabus. de disciplina christianorum. de x^cem cordis. Regula eiusdem de uita clericorum. de nuptiis et concupiscentia. et Aug. contra Julianum et contra duas epistolas pelagianorum et de sancta uirginitate in .1°. uol.

(late xv. cent.) Aug. ad simplicianum. Contra pelagium in 1°. vol. et alia.

C

Aug. contra Faustum in uno volumine.
Aug. de trinitate ,,
,, de Confessionibus ,,
,, de uerbis domini ,,

Aug. super genesim ad litteram et versus damasi pape in uno uol.

Epistole Aug. et Aug. contra interrogationes pelagij heretici in uno uol.

Aug. de penitentia. et unde malum. et de libero arbitrio et contra .v. hereses et de bono coniugali et pars quedam de perfectione iusticie. et hugo de archa noe in .1°. uol.

Aug. de bapt*ismo* paruul*orum*. et ad marcellinum et de unico bapt. de spiritu et littera et ad paulinum. et ẏponosticon. et contra pelagianos et de moribus ||
f. 1 *b* ecclesie. et contra epistolam manichei et Aug. de cura pro mortuis agenda in .1°. uol.

Aug. de doctrina christiana in uno volumine.

Aug. contra mendacium. et ad renatum de origine anime. contra libros vincentij. et ad petrum contra libros eiusdem vincentij. et ad uincentium uictorem. et contra perfidiam arrianorum. et contra aduersarios legis et prophetarum. et liber bestiarum. et Epistole Anselmi in .1°. uol.

Aug. de consensu euangelistarum et .11°. sermones eiusdem de iureiurando in .1°. uol.

Soliloquia Augustini et (erasure).

(late xv.) Aug. contra achademicos et de ordine monachorum.

D

Bernardus super cantica canticorum in uno uolumine.

Libri Bernardi. expositio scilicet super euangelium. Missus est angelus Gabriel. et de gradibus humilitatis et superbie. et de distincta uarietate monastice discipline et de gratia et libero arbitrio. et de diligendo deo. et exhortatio eiusdem ad milites templi. et libellus eiusdem ad Eugenium papam in uno uol.

Sermones Bernardi per anni circulum in uno uolumine.

Item Bernardus de gratia et libero arbitrio. et liber eiusdem ad ascelinum cardinalem de diligendo deo. et uersus hildeberti de missa in uno uol.

Item Bernardus de diligendo deo et sententia eius de Trinitate et de prescientia. de sacramento altaris. de quibusdam sacramentis fidei in uno uol.

Epistole Bernardi in uno uolumine.

Anselmus. cur deus homo. De conceptu uirginali. De monte humilitatis. De reparatione humane redemptionis. expositio euangelii Intrauit ihesus in quoddam castellum. et uita eiusdem. et Wimundus de corpore domini contra Berengarium in uno uol.

Libri Anselmi de incarnatione uerbi. Monologion. Proslogion eiusdem et contra eiusdem libri secundum et tertium et quartum capitulum oppositio cuiusdam. et responsio illius. Epistola ad Walerannum episcopum. Tractatus illius de ueritate. Tractatus illius de libero arbitrio. De casu diaboli. De concordia prescientie et predestinationis et gratie cum libero arbitrio. De similitudinibus. De gramatico. in uno uol.

Ailredus de spirituali amicicia et de institutione inclusarum in 1°. uol.

Liber sermonum illius qui sic incipit. Petis a me. etc. in uno uol.

Ailredus de oneribus ẏsaie in uno uol.

Ailredus de uita sancti edwardi. De generositate et moribus et morte regis ||

f. 2 *a* dauid. De uita sancti Niniani episcopi. De miraculis Haugustaldensis ecclesie in 1°. uol.

Epistole Ailredi in uno uolumine.

Ailredus de anima ,,

Speculum caritatis.

Epistole romanorum pontificum in uno volumine.

Epistole cẏpriani ,,

(late xv.) Alredus de fasciculo frondium.

E

Origenes super uetus testamentum in duobus voluminibus.

Rabanus super Matheum in uno vol.

Haimo super epistolas pauli ,,

Josephus de antiquitate ,,

Josephus de iudaico bello. et Ælredus de generositate regis dauid in uno uol.

Sentencie magistri Petri Lumbardi in uno uolumine.

F

Moralia beati Gregorij pape in Iob in quinque uoluminibus.

Greg. super Ezechielem in uno uol.

Liber pastoralis. et liber de tribus generibus homicidij. & liber de conflictu uiciorum & uirtutum in uno uol.

Liber Dialogi beati Gregorij in uno uol.

Liber quadraginta omeliarum ,,

Prima pars registri. et Aug. de uera religione. & Marsias in uno uol.

Secunda pars registri et liber de scientia dictandi in uno uol.

(late) de summa trinitate et fide catholica.

Robertus super apocalipsim in uno vol.

Liber sermonum & quedam excerpta de libris iustiniani & bestiarium in .1°. uol.

G

Ambrosius super lucam in uno uol.

,, super Beati immaculati ,,

,, de officijs et de sacramentis ,,

Epistole Ambrosij.

f. 2 *b* || Ambrosius de uirginibus & de Nabuthe & sermo eius de ieiunio & libellus Ricardi prioris de Beniamin et fratribus eius. De quibusdam partibus mundi. De vii^tem mirabilibus Rome. De quinque plagis anglie in uno uol.

Ambrosius de bono mortis. De fuga seculi. de uiduis. Exameron eiusdem. De penitentia & Cassiodorus de uirtutibus anime in uno uol.

Prima pars Ẏsidori ethimologiarum & expositio libri Donati grammatici & quedam deriuationes per alphabetum inchoantes & Regule uersificandi in uno uol.

Secunda pars Ẏsidori ethimologiarum & Ẏsidorus de quibusdam propriis nominibus veteris ac noui testamenti & eorum significationibus. & libellus Ẏsidori qui Sẏnonima apellatur in uno vol.

Johannes crisostomus super psalmum l. De muliere chananea. De reparatione lapsi. Aug. super mulierem fortem et vita duorum presbiterorum. Aug. de .xii. abusiuis et miraculum de corpore et sanguine domini & Beda super Thobiam. et Ẏsidorus de summo bono & diuersis uirtutibus in uno uol.

Liber beati Gregorij nazanzeni in uno uol.

Paralipomenon glosat*i* & quedam expositiuncule super epistolas pauli & sermones Babionis in uno uol.

Laurentius de consolatione amici & quedam decreta prm (paparum) & Ẏsagoge Johannicij in .1°. uol.

Epistole Senece in uno uol.

Sermones Mauricij qui sic incipiunt Festum super festum in uno uol.

Viginti octo sermones sancti Bernardi super cantica canticorum in uno uol.

H

Hugo de sacramentis in duobus voluminibus.

Hugo de contemptu mundi. Soliloquium eiusdem de cura anime. Item de uirginitate sancte marie. Solutio eiusdem cur non fiat coniugium inter eundem sexum & Didascalicon eiusdem in uno vol.

Tractatus Hugonis et Miracula de corpore & sanguine domini in uno uol.

[1] Hugo super ecclesiasten. & liber ecclesiasticorum dogmatum Gennadij et Eulogium magistri Johannis de Cornubia in uno vol.

Pannormia Ẏuonis carnotensis episcopi in uno vol.

(smaller) Item pannormia Ẏuonis. & Epistole Dindimi et Alexandri & Epistola Domini Bald*ewini* Abbatis de Forda. & Sermo de S. Thoma & S. Willelmo &
f. 3 *a* salubris admonitio cuiusdam sapien||tis quomodo de deo et de anima rudibus et minus peritis caute loquendum sit in .1°. vol.

Epistole Ẏuonis & Epistole Hildeberti episcopi cenomanni in uno vol.

Hugo super iherarchiam „

Robertus super matheum „

Robertus super leuiticum. Sermo magistri Roberti pullani de omnibus christiane uite necessarijs & libellus Ricardi prioris de Beniamin & fratribus eius & Regula S. Basilij in .1°. uol.

Epistole Mauricij in uno vol.

Libri Mauricij scilicet Specula monastice religionis & Apologia eiusdem & itinerarium pacis & Rithmus eiusdem & de translatione corporis S. Cuthberti in .1°. uol.

Lapidarium & quidam sermones & sentencie & compilationes in uno vol.

I

Beda super lucam in uno vol.
„ marcum „
„ de tabernaculo „
„ de ẏistoria anglorum „
„ de temporibus cum quibusdam cronicis eius „
„ de .xxx. questionibus & super esdram „
„ super samuelem „
„ super epistolas canonicas & super cantica canticorum „
„ de vita S. Cuthberti & Gregorius de transitu sancti Bede „

Libri de littera Anglica. duo

[1] (Note in late xv.) Sentencie hugonis.

K

Hẏstoria ecclesiastica in uno volumine.
Historia Egesippi ,,
,, Henrici ,,
,, de Ierusalem ,,
,, britonum ,,
Itinerarium Clementis ,,

Sermones magistri Gaufridi babionis & expositio in Johel prophetam & in Naum prophetam in uno volum.

Orosius de ormesta mundi. Historia Daretis de bello troianorum & versus Petri Abailardi ad filium & cronica de Anglia in .1°. vol. ||

f. 3 *b* Liber Aldelmi. quedam nomina & uerba de libro capitulorum. Hugo de Folieto de claustro materiali. Item de claustro anime. Inuectio Serlonis in .1°. vol.

Expositio euangelij Dixit Sẏmon petrus ad IHesum. Sermo de labore sanctorum & mercede. Sermo de ix[uem] mensibus conceptionis & viij diebus circumcisionis Christi. Sermo de sancto pascha. Collectiones sentenciarum & meditationum. Tractatus super quedam capitula de cant*icis* canticorum. Manipulus rerum & uerborum. in uno vol.

Expositio super cantica canticorum. Ambrosius super cantica canticorum. Expositio super Priscianum de constructionibus. Expositio super Apocalipsim. Item expositio super cantica canticorum. Glose Boecij & expositio breuis super quosdam psalmos in uno vol.

Johannes super decreta Gratiani in uno vol.
Corpus canonum ,,
Matheus glosatus ,,
Actus apostolorum glosati ,,

Boecius de trinitate. Liber catonis. passio S. Laurencij. prouerbia de libris poetarum. Vita S. marie egiptiace. Hildebertus de edificio anime. Item versus eiusdem. Quidam hẏmni. Odo de viribus herbarum. Marbodus de generibus lapidum. Passio S. Mauricij. Vita Tarsidis & alii uersus. Cosmographia Bernardi siluerij. Passio S. Thome. & alij uersus & dictamina in .1°. uol.

Uersarium de libris ethnicorum. Passio S. Laurencij. Argorismus in uno uol.

L

Vitas patrum. Vita S. Guthlaci. Liber qui dicitur formula uite honeste in 1°. uol.

Vita S. Godrici heremite in uno uol.
Johannes heremita in decem collationes ,,
Liber .xiiij[cim] collationum ,,
Prosper de uita actiua & contemplatiua & Diadema monachorum ,,
Liber Odonis ,,

Expositiuncula super uetus & nouum testamentum & quedam gesta in ecclesia pro passione domini. Aug. super psalmos & alie compilationes & regula splendescit in .1°. uol.

Liber Heraclidis episcopi qui dicitur paradisus & persecutio affricane provincie in .1°. vol.

Sentencie magistri Walteri que sic incipiunt. ferculum sibi fecit sal*em* in .1°. vol.
Sentencie que sic incipiunt. Dum medium silentium ,,
Regula Johannis cassiani ,,
Psalterium glosatum domini Æilredi abbatis in vno vol.
,, ,, ,, Ernaldi ,,

f. 4*a* Psalterium magistri Walteri glosatum in vno vol.
,, Thuroldi glosatum ,,
,, Radulfi barun ,,
,, Sẏmonis de sigillo ,,
,, paruum de probatorio ,,
,, Gaufridi dinant non ,,
,, Fulconis ,,
,, Willelmi de Rotelandia ,,
,, Jeronimi quod fuit Willelmi de berking ,,

Liber iustiniani de legibus in uno volum. M
,, medicinalis qui appellatur antidotarium ,,
Ẏsagoge Iohannicij ,,
Priscianus magnus ,,
,, de constructionibus ,,
Bernardus de xii. gradibus humilitatis. Sermones & sentencie utilissime. Apologeticum S. Bernardi. Interpretationes hebraicorum nominum in uno vol.
Sermones S. Bernardi qui sic incipiunt. Sancti per fidem & alie quedam sentencie in .1°. vol.
Expositio super Naum prophetam & super Johel. Sentencie & sermones & epistole plurimorum perutiles. Laurentius de creatione & operibus dei in uno vol.
Congestio diuersarum sentenciarum diuersis sancte catholice ecclesie causis congruentium & excerpta quedam de registro Gregorij ornate dicta in uno vol.
Sinonima ciceronis. quedam de compoto. regule uersificandi ,,
Rethorica ,,
Boecius de consolatione ,,
Ẏsagoge porphirij in cathegorias Aristotelis & alij libri dialectici in .1°. vol.
Liber de miraculis sancte marie in uno vol.

f. 4*b* Liber omeliarum in hẏeme in uno volum. N
,, in estate ,,
Passionale mensis octobris ,,
,, nouembris & decembris ,,
,, januarij ,,
Vita sancti Siluestri et aliorum sanctorum ,,
,, Ambrosij ,, ,,
Omelie in quadragesima ,,
Psalterium tripertitum ,,

Jeronimus super ẏsaiam in uno volum. O
,, .xij. prophetas in duobus volum.
,, Ieremiam et super Danielem in uno volum.
,, de hebraicis questionibus. De mansionibus filiorum israel. De distantijs locorum. De hebraicorum nominum interpretatione. De questionibus libri regum. De paralipomenis. De .x. temptationibus. De .vi. ciuitatibus fugitiuorum. De cantico debbore. De lamentationibus Ieremie. De edificio prud*entie*. Hugo de folieto de claustro anime. Jeronimus Gennadius Ysidorus de illustribus uiris. Cassiodorus de institutionibus diuinarum litterarum. Ailredus de standardo. de mappa in .1°. vol.

Bernardus super cantica canticorum. Jeremias glosatus. Item opuscula Bernardi & epistole & sententie plurimorum. Barbarismus glosatus. Epistole senece et pauli in uno volumine.

Sermones petri manducatoris. De ortu S. Cuthberti. Passio S. Thome Archiep. Cant. Miraculum de ẏmagine S. Marie. Vita S. Olaui in uno vol.

Quedam gesta saluatoris. Sermo Roberti pullani. Regula de quibusdam aduerbijs & questio de quadam constructione. Jeronimus contra Jouinianum. De locis misticis. Beda de arte metrica & de scematibus. Hugo de instructione nouiciorum. Epistola P*ra*tellici Abbatis ad episcopum suum & rescriptum episcopi in uno vol.

Vita S. Jeronimi & epistole eiusdem ,,

Sentencie magistri Roberti melodinensis blank

Sermones abbatis Werri in duobus volum.

Epistole Sẏdonij in uno vol.

f. 5 *a*

rubr. Libri glosati

P

Genesis	Gl. in 1°	vol.
Exodus	,,	,,
Ẏsaias	,,	,,
Item Ẏsaias	,,	,,
Job	,,	,,
Item Job	,,	,,
Duodecim prophete	,,	,,
Item .xij prophete	,,	,,
Sex prophete	,,	,,

Tobias & Judith Glosati & liber hester & Apocalipsis in 1° vol.

Cantica canticorum & epistole canonice Glosate in .1°. vol.

Matheus	gl. in 1°	vol.
Marcus	,,	,,
Item marcus	,,	,,
Lucas	,,	,,
Item lucas	,,	,,
Item lucas	,,	,,
Item Johannes	,,	,,
Item Johannes	,,	,,
Epistole canonice	,,	,,
Epistole pauli	,,	,,
Item epistola pauli	,,	,,
Apocalipsis	,,	,,

Item Apocalipsis & cantica canticorum Gl. in .1°.

Q

Liber usuum in duobus uoliminibus

Glosule super psalterium *Gilberti* pore in uno vol.

Quedam euangelia breuiter exposita. Exhortatio S. Bernardi ad Eugenium papam. Sententie patrum de vicijs & uirtutibus & phisica. Alia in uno vol.

Orationarium quod sic incipit Domine ihesu christe fili dei uiui. Bernardus de cantus proprietate. Hore de S. Maria. Jnstitutio capituli. Expositio super quosdam psalmos in uno vol.

Item orationarium quod sic incipit. Domine ihesu christe qui in hunc mundum. in 1° vol.

Sententie que sic incipiunt. Ne uelis tibi. et Prudentius in uno vol.

Quedam nominum et uerborum expositio in epistolas Pauli. Versus de christo et de sacramentis fidei. Quorundam patrum sermones in uno vol.

Encheridion & uersus cuiusdam de morte Roberti bloet episcopi lincolnie. & difficiliores partes ueteris ac noui testamenti in uno vol.

Quaedam commenta philosophie. quedam sententie pauli & ẏsaie. Flores quorundam euangeliorum. Aurea gemma. Epistola carnotensis episcopi mirifice utilitatis. Liber S. Patricij. Collatio trinitatis. S. Aug. a se ipso ad se ipsum.

Excerpsiones pannormie ẏuonis. Soliloquium Mauricij & quorundam uerborum interpretationes in .1°. vol.

Psalterium cum dimidiis uersibus & quedam orationes per rithmum in uno vol.

Libellus qui appellatur ẏmago mundi & alie sentencie ,,

Liber medicinalis qui fuit hugonis de Beuerl*aco*.

f. 5 *b*

Sentencie petri.

A Psalterium tripertitum
Corpus canonum. *Scintillarium*
Gratianus. *historica scolastica*
B*aldi*win*us in ij. uol.*

B Aug. de ciuitate dei
super psalterium .v
contra iulianum
de caritate
de perfectione iusticie
Encheridion duo
Aug. de gratia & libero arbitrio
de sermone domini in monte
de quantitate anime
super iohannem .xv.

C Regula S. benedicti
Aug. contra faustum
de trinitate
de confessionibus
de uerbis domini
super genesim ad litteram
Epistole aug.
Aug. unde malum
de baptismo p*aruulorum*
de doctrina christiana
contra mendacium
de consensu euangeliorum
contra Achademicos
Soliloquium augustini .xiiij

D Bernardus super cantica canticorum
Libri Bernardi
Bernardus ad papam eugenium
Sermones bernardi
Aeldredus de spirituali amicicia
Sermones aeldredi
Vita S. Edwardi
Epistole aelredi
Aelredus de anima
Epistole romanorum pontificum

Epistole cypriani
Epistole bernardi
Speculum caritatis
Bernardus de diligendo deum. xiiij

E Origenes super uetus testamentum in .ii°. uol.
Rabanus super matheum
Hamo super epistolas pauli
Iosephus de antiquitate
Iosephus de iudaico bello
erasure.
Itinerarium clementis .vij.

F Moralia in .v. voluminibus
Gregorius super Ezechielem
Pars prima registri
,, secunda
Cur deus homo
Libri Anselmi
Epistole iuonis
Liber pastoralis
Liber .xl. omeliarum
Dialogus gregorii
Robertus super apocalipsim
Liber sermonum. .xvj.

G Ambrosius de fide
f. 6*a* super Lucam
beati immaculati
de officiis
de uirginibus
Epistole ambrosii
Bernardus super cantica
Exameron
Egesippus
Iohannes crisostomus
Isẏdorus in ii°. uol.
Gregorius nazanzenus
Laurentius
Epistole senece
Sermones festum super festum
Paralipomenon. glos. xvij

H hugo de sacramentis in ii° uol.
contemptu mundi
Tractatus hugonis
Robertus super matheum
Hugo super ecclesiasten
Sermones Mauricii

Epistole Mauricii
Panormia ẏuonis
Item panormia ẏuonis
hugo super ierarchiam
Robertus super leuiticum
Liber lapidum
Sermones o quam xiiij

I Beda super lucam
marcum
tabernacula
historia Anglorum
Beda de temporibus
xxx. questionibus
super samuelem
cantica canticorum
Vita S. Cuthberti
Compotus. *paulus heremita.*
historia fulcheri
britonum xiij

K Epistole pauli glos.
Psalterium
Matheus
Marcus Sẏdonius
Lucas
Iohannes
Apocalipsis & actus apostolorum Gl.
Epistole canonice Gl.
Missale. passio s. Thome
Psalterium abbatis. Orosius
h*i*storia Ecclesiastica
Iohannes super decreta
Boetius de consolationibus
Sententie quid est tibi mare
Collectiones. Item collectiones .xix.

L Vitas patrum. Vita s. godrici
Decem collationes heremitarum
Quatuordecim collationes
Exceptiones. Babio.
Diadema monachorum
Sententie magistri Walteri
Sententie que sic incipiunt. Dum medium silentium.

f. 6 *b*

Iohannes cassianus Paradisus .xij.
Psalteria .xx.

M

Medicinalis aurea
Pricianus magnus
Pricianus de constructionibus
Sententie que sic incipiunt Cum complerentur
Sermones. Timenti dominum
Retorica. Boetius de trinitate
Boetius de consolatione. Epistole imperiales
Isagoge porfilij. Claudianus
Liber odonis (erasure). Aldelmus
Sinonima ciceronis
Isagoge iohannicii
Sententie petri et med'ile xviij
Sententiole. Sermones bernardi Sancti p. et Libri omeliarum ii°.

N

Passionale mensis ianuarii
octobris
nouembris
Vita S. Silvestri. Vita S. Ambrosii
Omelie in xl^{ma}. viij

O

Ieronimus super ysaiam
xii. prophetas in ii°. vol.
Gregorius super cantica
Afferte domino (in erasure)
Cantica uersibus expressa Item cantica canticorum
Opuscula hildeberti
Ieronimus super danielem
contra iouinianum. Epistole ieronimi
Sermones uerri in ii°. uol.
Versarium Reinaldi. Ieremias gl.
Ieronimus de ebraicis questionibus. Sermones petri manducatoris .xvij

P

Genesis Gl. Exodus Gl.
Duodecim prophete iii. Sex prophete
Ẏsaẏe duo. Job duo. Tobias
Lucas tres Marcus Matheus .ii.
Iohannes tres Epistole pauli .ii.
Apocalipsis i. Actus apostolorum
Cantica canticorum. Epistole canonice
Item cantica canticorum xxvij

Q

Gillebertus super psalterium. Liber usuum
Liber arnulfi
Orationaria .ii°. sententie
Miracula s. marie
Expositio in epistolas pauli
Sententie Gl. Medicinale

Liber interpretationum hebraicorum nominum
Collectiones
Scintillarium (erased)
Apocalipsis glosatus
Sermones. Gaudeamus
Gillebertus super cantica. xvij.

This second list is mainly a shorter *replica* of the first: at the end of each class is a note of the number of volumes in it.

35. Q. B. 18.

ITINERARIUM JOH. MANDEVILLE, ETC.

Paper, $8\frac{7}{8} \times 6\frac{1}{8}$, ff. 160, 35 and 27 lines to a page. Cent. xv.

Given by Mr Man.

Binding: original boards covered with brown leather of cent. xvii, xviii.

Collation: i^6 (1 and 6 parchment: 5 cancelled) ii^2 || a^{18} b^{16} c^{16} d^{14} = 64 leaves || a^{12} b^{14} c^{12}–f^{12} g^{12} (12 cancelled) 85 leaves || ii^8 (1, 4, 5, 8 parchment: 2, 4, 5, 6, 7 cancelled).

Provenance. Probably Durham. There is a xvth cent. table of contents on f. v *a*.

In isto libro continentur. Itinerarium
Johannis Maundevill Militis.
Item habetur de Machometo capitulo .xl.
Item Narraciones de gestis Romanorum moralizate.

The 2nd leaf of the text begins: *crucem domini Judei.*

Contents:

1. f. ii.–iv. contain Latin and English notes on the power and glory of God, of cent. xvii.
   ff. vi, vii, are blank.
2. Itinerarium Johannis Maundevill . . . . f. 1
   In 88 sections: in Latin.
   Colophon, f. 64 *a*.
   Expl. Itinerarium Domini Joh. de Maundevill Militis de Mirabilibus Mundi.
   f. 65 *b* is blank.
3. Gesta Romanorum . . . . Part II. f. 1

Fifty-eight stories, not corresponding to the contents of any one MS. described in Oesterley's edition of the *Gesta* (Berlin 1872) but most resembling Cod. Harl. 2270 (described by him p. 187).

I append the list of Emperors in the Jesus MS. and the corresponding numbers of the tales in the Harley MS.

		Harl.
1	Ancelmus	1
2	Dioclitianus	2
3	Leo	3
4	Lolius	—
5	Ganterus	4
6	Freudricus	5
7	Freudicus	6
8	Felicianus	7
9	Domicius	8 (Lucius)
10	Dioclicianus	9
11	Heculeus	11 (Betoldus)
12	Pompeius	12
13	Adrianus	13
14	Fredrian	15
15	Eadices	(Caclides)
16	Antonius	24
17	(B)enonius	26
18	Andeonius	28 (Andronicus)
19	Iouinianus	29
20	Phebus	31
21	Cesar	32
22	Cranpadius	33 (Lamp.)
23	Insennanus	34 (Ensonn.)
24	Ancelmus	22
25	Lepodius	16
26	(F)elliculus	—
27	Leucippus	—
28	(P)ollonius	48
29	Agio	69 the two wounds
30	Adrianus	20 (soldier Porfirius)
31	Theodocius	21
32	Andronicus	25
33	Mobilissimus rex	—
34	Antonius	27
35	Mamertius	35
36	Ardemius	36
37	Plebeus	37
38	Barlaam (unicorn)	
39	Alexander	65
40	Eraclius	66
41	Fulgencius	67
42	Archillaus	68
43	Eufemianus	69
44	Iosias	70
45	Pollemius	71
46	Poemius	73
47	Fulgencius	74
48	Domicianus	75
49	Antonius	76
50	Andronius	77
51	Teobaldus	78
52	Mireus	79
53	Olimpius	80
54	Innianus	Lion with thorn 100
55	Darius	81
56	Aquileus	82 (Menelaus)
57	Euclides (De Gwydone et lapide precioso)	94, 102
58	Pancrasius	84

The last quire of the volume contains two cancel-pages of Maundeville, one (loose) corresponding to f. 24*a* (§ xxix), the other to f. 56*a* (§ lxxiii).

On the last parchment leaf is:

Sumr. thome rysyng du..............a Orforthe.

36. Q. B. 19.

ROBERTI LINCOLNIENSIS SUMMA JUSTITIAE.

Vellum, $8\frac{1}{2} \times 6$, ff. 218, double columns of 36 lines each. Cent. xv.

There is no donor's name. The name Henry Murgetrode occurs at the end of the index.

Binding: original boards, not covered with skin: rebacked: strap and pin fastening gone: mark of staple near right edge of front cover, underneath the clasp.

The second leaf of the table begins *de remediis:* the second leaf of text 22 *nulla est.*

Collation: a^4 (wants 1) b^{12}–k^{12} l^8 m^{12}–s^{12} t^{16} (13, 14, 16 cancelled) u^4 (3, 4 cancelled).

Other MSS. of this work are Balliol cccxx, Lincoln (Oxf.) cv, Peterhouse 89, Camb. Univ. Ff. iii 24, all of cent. xv.

It is in ten parts.

37. Q. B. 20.

LECTURE-NOTES BY FRANC. STIRLING.

Paper, $8\frac{5}{8} \times 7$, ff. 189, 52 lines to a full page. Cent. xvii (1669).

Contents:

The heading on p. 1 runs thus:

In generalia Philosophiae Theoremata vulgo dicta Metaphysica Praefatio dictata a Magistro Gulielmo Patersone et a me Francisco Stirling conscripta 1669.

The dates of the lectures run to March, 1671.

They are followed by

Axiomata Mori de immortalitate animae in English, the names of the constellations, and three pages of Theses.

38. Q. B. 21.

S. GREGORII NAZIANZENI OPERA.

Vellum, 8×6, ff. 119, 25 lines to a page. Cent. xii.

Binding: modern skin over the old boards: formerly had strap and pin fastenings. Given by Mr Man.

Provenance. Hexham. On the bottom of f. 1 is

Liber sancti Andree de Hextildesham (xv.).
The old title on the fly-leaf is Apologij gregorii cum aliis (xv.).

Collation: Thirteen quires of 8, one of 6, the last of 8 (+ 8*).

Contents:

On f. 1 is a title in red in 9 lines.

In hoc corpore continentur libri .viii[to]. gregorii episcopi nazanzeni. id est. Apologeticus liber unus. De epiphaniis siue de natali domini liber unus. De luminibus siue secundis epiphaniis liber unus. De pentecosten de spiritu sancto liber unus. In semet ipso de agro liber unus. De ieremie dictis presente imperatore apud quem intercedit pro quodam periclitante liber unus. De reconciliatione monachorum liber unus. De grandinis uastatione cum pater episcopus reticeret liber unus.

Incipit Prefatio RVFINI AD (A)PRONIANVM . . . . . f. 1
Apologeticus . . . . 2 *b*
de epiphaniis (orat. 38, ed. Par.) . . . . 39 *b*
de luminibus (orat. 39, ed. Par.) 50
de pentecoste (orat. 44, ed. Par.) 61
de semetipso (orat. 28, ed. Par.) 71
de Ieremie dictis (orat. 17, ed. Par.) 82
de reconciliatione monachorum (orat. 12, ed. Par.) 89
de grandinis uastatione (orat. 15, ed. Par.) . . . . . . 100 *b*
Ends on 110 *a*, the verso is blank.
Incipit tractatus in canone misse et de differentiis in faciendis crucibus et de pluribus aliis necessariis, scilicet que sit causa misse que differentia quis finis que uirtus quis ordo que ratio que utilitas, a Ricardo abbate ecclesie premonstrati ordinis editus.
In uirtute sancte crucis 111

Ends on 119 *a*, verso blank: in a different hand, 26 lines to a page. The initials to the orations of Gregory are large and bold: blue and red are the prevailing colours: the writing is very good.

39. Q. B. 23.

LECTURE-NOTES BY FR. STIRLING.

Paper, 8 × 6, ff. 132, various numbers of lines to a page. Cent. xvii (1668).

Contents:

Structurae Supplementum.

Dictatum a magistro Gulielmo Patersone et a me Francisco Stirlingo sub ejus feuda versante (erasure).

Con Anno 1668 scriptum 10°. novem.

It is a system of Logic. On p. 200 is a note.

Finem Logicis imposuimus 19 Calen. Janua: 14 die Decembris anno domini 1669 paulo ante horam undecimam.

Four pages of notes follow.

40. Q. B. 24.

ACTA APOSTOLORUM CUM GLOSSA.

Vellum, $8\frac{1}{2} \times 5\frac{1}{2}$, ff. 114, 17 lines of text to a page. Cent. xii.

Original boards re-covered: chain-mark at bottom of last leaf. Given by Mr Man.

Collation: i^{2} a^{8}–n^{8} o^{10} (10 gone).

Probably from Durham: f. 2 begins (text) *Quibus et* (gloss. *humanitas a diuinitate*). I do not find it in the old Catalogues.

It is very well written, with plain red or green initials; on f. 113 is Explicit liber actuum apostolorum liber $\overset{\Omega}{\overline{\text{VIII}}}$. D . C (for habet v(ersus) $\overline{\text{III}}$. D . C.)

41. Q. B. 25.

SPECULUM RELIGIOSORUM, ETC.

Vellum, $8\frac{1}{2} \times 5\frac{3}{4}$, ff. 176, 37 lines to a page. Cent. xv, xiv, and xiii.

Given by Mr Man. Binding: the original wooden boards covered with newer leather: formerly fastened with strap and pin.

Provenance: most likely Durham: it contains a tract by Uthred of Bolton, who was a monk of Durham, and Prior of Finchale in 1371. Not in *Catt. Vett.*

Collation: a^{12} b^{12} c^{8} d^{12} || e^{6} f^{8} g^{8} || h^{12}–k^{12} l^{8} m^{10} n^{10} o^{6} (wants 3, 4, 6) || p^{10} || q^{8} r^{8} s^{8} (wants 7, 8) t^{2} u^{4} v^{6}.

Contents:

1. Speculum Religiosorum . . . . f. 1
   Cent. xv.: imperfect, beginning in c. 26: ends on 44 *a*,

followed by a table of the chapters: at the bottom of the page is:

orate pro anima Johannis de Hallughton.

On the verso, otherwise blank, are six lines on S. Mary Magdalen, beginning

Fletque rigatque pedes domini tergitque capillis,

and a xvith cent. name Robert Horsley.

2. A Table of the contents of a volume, not the present one 45
Cent. xiv. a list of 24 sermons and the *Capitula* of a *Summa de vicijs* in 131 chapters.

3. A Tract on ecclesiastical discipline . . . . . . 46 *b*
In another hand, of cent. xv.: double columns of 38 lines each
Inc. *De nocturna illusione.* Cum nocturna illusio sit una species luxurie: the last chapter is *de celestia gloria:* ends on 65 *a* col. 1, col. 2 (blank) is cut off, 65 *b*, 66 were blank: on 66 *a* is a rude drawing of a crucifix: on 65 *b* are 5 lines on England.

Anglia terra ferax et fertilis angulus orbis.

4. Tabula super regulam S. Benedicti 67
Capitula on f. 67: text f. 68, cent. xv. 37 lines to a page.

5. Tabula super librum B. Bernardi de precepto et dispensacione 88
Compilata a magistro Vthredo Boltoñ (the name added to the colophon on 101 *b*).

6. Tabula breuis super libellum dictum *Abbas uel Prior* . . 102 *b*

7. Tabula breuis super constituciones benedictinas . . . 108

8. Quomodo et processus qualiter Judas postquam tradidit Ihesum uenit ad matrem suam et qualiter consuluit eam et noluit ab....
Inc. Postquam Iudas tradidit Ihesum Iudeis.
The story of Judas and the cock, which also occurs in Q. D. 4: the same text, ending 'laqueo se suspendit sicque inter celum et terram periit quod magistrum suum dei vnigenitum saluatorem omnium credencium tradidit. Expl. miserabilis finis Iude traditoris Ihesu Christi.'
Added in a xvth cent. hand in col. 2 of . . . . . . 109 *a*

9. Regula beati Benedicti.
In the hand of nos. 4—7: and imperfect in c. 73 . . . 110

10. Articuli 5—14 on feudal rights of Durham (?) . . . 132
Added in cent. xv, xvi, on a leaf originally blank: imperfect, beginning in art. 4.
de terra uel feodo prioris dimidiabunt inter episcopum et priorem sine dificultate.

11. Constitution of the Abbots of S. Alban's, S. Mary of York, and Chester, for the Benedictines in England . . . 133
Cent. xiv.
Followed by two notes, one from Lanfranc, one on the rule of S. Benedict: of cent. xv. . . . . 141 *b*
142 *b* is blank.

12. Extracts:

(*a*) Hoc autem non te lateat Petre, quid uir dei inter tot miracula 143

(*b*) Plurimi nequaquam pleniter intelligentes (on the Rule). 143

(*c*) nota in rosario .xxvij. q. .ij. de eo quod dicitur in regula monachorum, monachus recedens de monasterio etc. 144

In a hand of cent. xv.: 34 lines to a page.

13. Meditations.

Incipiunt meditaciones excitatiue compunctionis ex sacre scripture et sanctorum sentenciis compilate presertim ex sentenciis beati Augustini beati Bernardi et venerabilis Anselmi.

Memento miser homo. In 9 chapters: a table at the end 145

14. Meditacio diuine laudis et spei uenie prouocatiua composita a dicto magistro Willelmo monacho et doctore . . . 150 *b*

I find no previous mention of William.

Memor fui dei et delectatus sum.

15. Meditacio diuini amoris desideratiua composita ab eodem . 153 *b*

Memento mei deus.

16. Meditacio composita a domino Vtredo monacho Dunelmensi et sacre pagine professore ad excitandum hominem cognoscere semetipsum.

Domine recogitabo tibi omnes annos . . . . . . 156 *b*

In a larger hand: 31 lines to a page: a later note is added on 163 *a*.

17. Notes of ordinances concerning the order 164

Diffinitum est quod abbates singuli et priores gestu et habitu regulariter se habentes.

Nine paragraphs, cent. xv.

18. Copia litere domini Bernardi de Genebreda Prioris prioratus de Longauilla ord. Cluniac. dioc. Rothomag. de reuocatione censurarum constitutionum Benedicti Pape xii^mi^ presidentibus in capitulo prouinciali anglie die Marcurii prox. post fest. Nativ. B. Marie celebrato apud Northampton anno domini mccc. xliij°. cent. xv. 165

19. Innocencius IIII etc. dilecto filio Priori Dunelm., giving him power to dispense with strict observance of the Rule: ends. Istud est in domo nostra bullatum et est censuracio facta ab eodem Innoc. Abbatibus de Ebor. et de Seleby 168

20. Informacio ad computandum algorismum.

In the hand, I think, of no. 10: added . . . . . 168 *b*

21. Ordinaciones facte in Annuali Capitulo Dunelm. by Prior Wessyngton in 1417.

Cent. xv. 13 paragraphs . . . . 169 *b*

23. Littere Mag. Rostandi de inquisicione pecunie e. Archidiac. Dunelm.

Cent. xiii. He was nuncius of Alexander 171

The first letter is dated York 2 Non. Ap. a.d. 1256.
There are ten documents in all, ending on 176 *a*: f. 176 is glued to the cover.

42. Q. B. 27.

Prosodia Sacerdotum.

Vellum, $6\frac{3}{4} \times 4\frac{1}{2}$, ff. 47, double columns of 35 lines each. Cent. xv, after 1443.

The donor's name does not appear.

Binding: stamped leather, on the front side miscellaneous stamps are used, principally large fleurs-de-lys with an irregular quatrefoil in the *L.* upper corner: on the other cover dolphins enclosing 3 panels: (*a*) and (*c*) En dieu(?) | mafye, (*b*) a large Lombardic P: outside all a band of flowers in lozenges: one brass clasp.

Collation: a[6] b[10] (wants 10) c[8] d[8] e[8] f[8].

Contents:

1. Prosodia Sacerdotum 1

This is a table of all the words in the lessons, etc., for the whole year, in which mistakes in prosody were likely to be made. The quantity of the penultimate syllable is indicated by an *l* for *longa*, *b*=breuis, *s*=accent *subleuatus* on the last syllable, *d* for a *depressura* of the accent on the last. There is a fair border on f. 1 *a* of English work, and other partial borders occur, but the ornament is not remarkable. In the part relating to the *Proprium Sanctorum* we have the usual Sarum English Saints, with special emphasis on S. Frideswide: her feast, octave, translation, *Dominica infra Octauam*, and *Per Octauam:* following this, and immediately preceding the *Commune Sanctorum*, is *Inuencio fratrum*.

2. A Chronology from 1370 to 1443 . . . . 46 *b*

In another hand, in red and black: the Sunday Letter, Golden Number, etc., are given for every year, and a good many commemorations of events, recorded in English, as follows: italics indicate rubrication.

1377		d	10	3	m	*Coronacion of kẏng Richard.*
1379		b	12	10	a	y[e] town of gravysend brent.
1380	Ꝃ	g	13	7	*m*	*Rẏsẏng of ẏ[e] commons of Kent.*
1381						ye girt erth mouẏng.

1382 *Beschop of norwẏch goyng into flanders.*
1387 ye risẏng of .v. lordẏs.
1394 *Qwen anne dẏede.*
1395 Qwen Isabel crounede.
1397 *Erle of arndel died.*
47 *a* 1399 Kẏng herri •4• Crownede.
1400 *A gret dreth.*
1401 humbildumbil batel and douglas takyn ther.
1402 *Stella comota* (=*cometa*) *&* • 8 • *freris hangyde.*
1403 Batel of Schrewsberẏ.
1404 *Bẏschop of ȝorke behedede.*
1405 An huge frost 16 wokẏs.
1407 *Erle of northumberland be hedid.*
1409 þe kẏngs sonnys ẇbet in eschape.
1411 *þe noble first alaied.* (=allayed).
1412 her Oolde castel brake prisone.
1413 *Crownẏng of kẏng harri • v • & rẏsẏng of olde castel knyȝt.*
1414 her was herflede (Harfleur) be schegẏde.
1416 Sege of cane & cumyng of þe emperur into þis londe.
1417 *Oolde castel was hongyde.*
1419 Qwen Kateryne weddẏde.
1420 *Crownẏnge of þ^{e} quene.*
1421 Bẏrth of kẏnge herrẏ • vj^{te} •
1423 *Sir will' taylliour prest brent.*
1425 a discencion betwen london & bẏchope of winchester.
1426 *In þis ȝer þ^{e} sam bẏschope was made Cardenal'.*
1429 Crownẏng of kẏng herri þe vj. at westm'.
47 *b* 1431 *Crounyng of owr kẏng a^{t} paryche.*
1434 • 15 • wokis duringe a gret frost.
1436 *þ^{e} duke of burgun was driuin fro calice & his bastil brent.*
1437 þe rate of of london brike brake & fel downe.
1441 þe duchese of gloucestre was put to penance.

The name of Richarde Smith, as owner, occurs on f. 43 *b*.

43. Q. D. 1.

MISC. MEDICA.

Paper, $8\frac{3}{4} \times 6$, ff. 164, 40 lines to a page. Cent. xv.
Binding: leather of cent. xviii, over old boards.
Collation: i^{4} a^{12} b^{16} c^{6} (+ 6*) d^{12} e^{14} (wants 14) f^{6} (wants 5) g^{8} h^{8} i^{12} k^{12} l^{14} (1 inserted) m^{12} n^{12} o^{12} ii^{4}.

Contents:

wele it is good tresore. kepe it welle as yowre owne lyff ffor i haue made to helpe & hele of yowre body . . . . . 126 *b*

Euery man beste and fowle hayth • iiii • hum*er*us.

De quatuor infirmitatibus corperum vbi insurgunt, in English . . 128 *a*

On the nine pulses, in English . . . . 129 *a*

To wete & to knowe ye veynes off blode letynge . . . . . 131 *a*

On the pure complexions . . . . 134 *b*

De numeris ossium ac venarum et dencium in humanis corporibus . 135 *a*

Miscellaneous receipts in English . . . . 135 *a*

here begynnyth a nobil tretyse made of a physy<cy>an John of burdews for medysyn ageyn þe pestylens euylle . . . . . 137 *a*

Expl. tract. Joh. de burgall editus contra morbum pestilencie qui est morbus epidimialis anno domini mill^{mo} ccc^{mo} nonagesimo.

Receipts in English . . . . 139 *a*

Receipts and notes on the treatment of wounds, in Latin . . 151 *a*

A tract in Latin, with invocation of God's help in a rubric at the beginning, but no title.

Medicina pro corpore humano finaliter componuntur . . . . 155 *b*

Receipts in English and Latin, in several hands . . . . . 157 *b*

There are four vellum fly-leaves of cent. xiv at each end containing records of cases.

f. 1 *a*. *Inc*. Predict. comes Gloucestr. et Herford et macle.

1 *b*. Norff. Joh. de Manteby et Petrus frater eius petit uersus Robertum de Manteby duas partes quatraginta et sex mesuag., etc.

2 *b* mentions Thorp. Matelask. Stenekeye. Manyngtone. Salle. Wethyngham.

Ib. Will. de Ancrenges tenuit Baron. de ffolkestan.

3 *b*. Noting. Herb. de Rysele, Rob. de Heyle ... ad respond. Prior de Symplyngham.

4 *a*. Rad. Basset et Joh. le Heyward ... ad respond. Will^{o} de (?) Tÿfford persone med. Eccl. de Weledon.

Ib. Placita apud Westm. de quindena Pasch. coram O. de Weylond et soc. suis Anno v. v. E. sextodecimo.

f. 161 *a*. Joh. de Hilde tulit breue quod vocatur quare impedit ... about the Church of N.

161 *b*. (Rob.) fil. Ric^{l} de Adeston etc. ad resp. Thome Ep^{o} hereford.

162 *a*. Tho. de Aschamton.

162 *b*. Leycestr. All in French.

163 *b*. Latin resumed. Margaret, widow of Hugh de Wynestuwe petit uersus abbatem de oseneye.

These leaves are a good deal torn.

44. Q. D. 2.

DIOSCORIDES, ETC.

Vellum, $8\frac{1}{2} \times 6\frac{1}{2}$, ff. 159, varying number of lines to a page. Cent. xii, xiii.

Binding: original white skin over boards: strap and pin fastening. Given by Mr Man.

Provenance: Durham: on f. 2 *a* is written (cent. xii, xiii)

Liber sancti Cuthberti de Dunelm°. In darker ink, Ex dono magistri Herberti medici. Diascorides. Liber de natura lapidum. Exceptiones de libro pauli. Dicta quedam Petri alfunsi. Quedam pars prisciani de accentibus. Pars libri aurelii ambrosii.

In a hand of cent. xv, xvi

Contenta {
diascorides per modum alphabeti de virtutibus herbarum et compositione olerum.
Item lapidarius quidam liber de natura lapidum per modum alphabeti.
Priscianus de accentibus.
Item notabilia quedam in libro primo.
2^{dus} 7^{i} ffe.

Below this is an index of cent. xvii.

On f. 3 *a* in a hand of cent. xv,

Diascorides • liber de natura lapidum O. 2^{dus} 7^{i} ffe.

In *Cat. Vet.* p. 8 (in the Catalogue of cent. xii) we find

Exceptiones de Libro Pauli.
Priscianus de accentibus.
Parabolae Petri Amphulsi.
Liber Aurelii Ambrosii.
Liber Diascoridis.
Liber de Natura Lapidum in uno volumine.

In the Catalogue of 1391 (p. 33)

Libri Medicinae.

O. Diascorides. Liber de Nat. Lap. Exerciones de lib. Pauli. Dicta quaedam Petri Alfonsi. Quaedam pars Priciani de accent. ii. fo. *leporum ventres.*

The first cover is lined with part of a leaf (unfinished, and without the intended musical notes) of a service book containing lessons and antiphons from Isaiah, beautifully written, of cent. xiii.

Collation: a^4 (+4* blank) b^4 c^8 (wants 7) vi^8 vii^{10} viii^8 ix^4 x^8 xi^8 xii^8 xiii^4 (wants 2) xiv^8 xv^8 xvi^8 xvii^8 xviii^{10} xix^{10} xx^{10} xxi^8 xxii^6 (wants 6, blank) d^8 e^6 (wants 5, blank: 6 was the cover).

Contents:

Three receipts, in Latin, for dyeing the hair . . . . . . f. 1 *a*
f. 1 *b* is blank : f. 2 *a* contains the table of contents cited above.
Pauli liber de cura egritudinum parcium tocius corporis: et primum de allopicia et toffia siue caluitio. Cent. xii, xiii . . . . 2 *b*
This tract relates only to the hair and its diseases.
f. 5 is blank.
Dicta philosophorum (per Petrum Alfunsum), without title . . 6
In four chapters beginning respectively (cent. xiii, xiv)

1. Animo melius distincta seruantur.
2. Cum quidam stolidus audiente so*crate* diceret.
3. Apius claudius crebro solebat dicere.
4. Cato octogesimum sextum agens annum.

Septem facetie et septem rusticitates . . . . 8 *b*
f. 9 *a* is blank save for two late receipts.
f. 10 *a* is blank.
Priscianus de accentibus. Cent. xii, xiii . . . . . . 10 *b*
ff. 15 *b* and 16 are blank.
Dioscorides de uirtutibus herbarum. Cent. xii, xiii 17
30 lines to a page: very good hand. The quires are numbered on their first leaves VI–XXII. The hand varies considerably in appearance. There are in some instances marks on the first leaf of the quire, indicative of the portion of the text which it contains. Thus quire X, containing parts of letters B and C, is marked c. ii: XI is c. XXV: XII is can. et ed. (it extends from Cardamus to Ediosmum): XIV is F. j J. ij (Fel to Iacinctus): XV is ꝛ. i et o. j ī lacþ l. (Ius—Litargirum): XVII is m. ij (Mandragora—Oleum): XXI is ꝛ. i v. j (Thalapsium—Vinum).
The text ends on f. 145 *a*: a slightly later extract on the intellect: ff. 145 *b*–147 *a* contain late receipts (cent. xvii): f. 147 *b* is blank.
Liber de natura lapidum: in French verse. Cent. xii, xiii, double columns 148
Headed on top margin: Incip. lapidarius. Sancti spiritus assit nobis gratia. Damante.

Co nus demustre laimant. D*eus* ot en tere icel semblant. Ki en la nuit done luur. Co est en nostre tenebrur. Adamas ad de fer culur. Et cristal la resplendur. Demustrance del creatur. Quo il nus traist denfein a luur. Si cum la pere trait le fer. IHU crist nus traist denfer.

The poem extends from Aimant to Trisites, in alphabetical order. On f. 158 is the Epilogue, which runs thus:

Dirrund cil qui ues conuister*unt*. Puet cel estre quo fables sunt. Ne que aureie dunt penser. Quant Jo desesperai et lesuei. Mais sil se uolunt p*re*penser et les peres esp*er*ment*er*. lur creatur aurer*unt*. pur les miracles quo il u*er*runt. Que il posa pur tote gent. as peres medicinem*ent*. En surq*ue* tut q*ua*tre maneres. mustrat medicine des peres. Pur le tocher. pur le porter. pur le beiure. pur les guarder. Ces quatre maneres i posad. Deus grant signifiance ad. E co dirrai en lautre liure. Se IHU xpist me leisse uiure. kar co ert tut allegorie. de IHU crist le fiz marie. Tut co serra diuinite. quen lautre liure ert demustre. E al *pro*loge musterum. de qui auctorite t*ra*itum. E deus mait al come*n*cer. e al finer et al *tra*iter. Ci fine li liure t*er*restre. e commence li celestre.

There follow in a hand of the same pencil some paragraphs on the polishing of precious stones, extending to the end of col. 1, f. 158 *b*.

45. Q. D. 3.

REPERTORIUM SUPER SPECULUM HISTORIALE VINCENTII DE BELUACE.

Vellum, $7\frac{3}{4} \times 5\frac{3}{8}$, ff. 264, 32 lines to a page. Cent. xv.

Given by Mr Man.

Binding: stamped leather of xvth century (re-backed and paper boards inserted: formerly had two clasps): the stamps used are four: (1) square, a Paschal Lamb and flag face to *L.*; (2) square, a lion walking to *L.*; (3) lozenge-shaped, a bird with raised wings facing *R.*; (4) circular within a square, a hare seated facing *R.*

Collation: a^8-r^8 s^{10} t^8–z^8 aa^8–ff^8 gg^8 (4–8 blank, gone).

Provenance: Durham. On the 3rd fly-leaf is the following inscription:

L. Repertorium super speculum historiale cum contratabula 2° fo. *cat.*

then in another hand:

Iste liber assignatur Nono (? nouo) Armariolo in Claustro Dunelm. Ecclesie per venerabilem patrem magistrum Johannem Auklande priorem eiusdem ecclesie.

The first leaf has a good border of English work in gold, blue, green, orange and pink: a columbine in the initial: a good partial border on f. 5 *a*.

Contents:

Prologue addressed to Simon, Cardinal of S. Prisca, by John haut furey, presbyter; this must have been Simon d'Archiac, Archbp of Vienne, made Cardinal in 1320, d. 1320 or 1323 . . . f. 1 *a*

The prologue is in three divisions, explanatory of the plan of the work.

Text . . . . 5 *a*

A list of the headings, in the nominative case, in 4 cols. on a page, with a prefatory note . . . . 246 *b*

A list of the 'flores' or extracts contained in the Speculum Historiale, with a prefatory note . . . . 263 *b*

The table seems well constructed and full, and would very likely be worth printing.

46. Q. D. 4.

ELUCIDARIUS, ETC.

Vellum, $6\frac{3}{4} \times 4\frac{1}{2}$, ff. 269 + 5 fly-leaves, varying number of lines to the page. Cent. xv, and xii, xiii.

Belonged to the College in 1664.

Binding: red skin over boards: has had strap and pin fastening.

Collation: i^2 || a^8–i^8 || k^8–s^8 t^{10} u^8–y^8 z^4 (3, 4 blank, gone) || i^8–iv^8 v^8 (+ 8*) vi^8–x^8 || 2^2 (+ 2*) = 269 + 5.

Provenance. On a fly-leaf at the beginning (cent. xv, xvi):

Istum librum e tra t dus Joh. Walsh.
Constat magistro Thome Audley et Roberto Swann.
Fortitudo et honor ...

On a fly-leaf at the end, in another earlier hand:

Memorandum quod iste liber constat domino Johanni Thrope pro quo habet in plegio librum de gestu romanorum domini A lax.

This is written over a pencilled list of expenses, of which the following are legible:

ad goldyngton
ad lytlyngton
pro cor(i)o.
ad unum par calig.
goldyngton.

... iiij[d] di pro tribus.
paribus sotularium.

The last fly-leaf is part of a will of cent. xv, relating to Northampton, of which a transcript is given on p. 74.

Contents:

On the recto of the 2nd fly-leaf at the beginning of the book is a long table of contents, written in cent. xv, which I transcribe, adding numbers of the leaves, etc.

In hoc libello in nouo pergameno continentur quinque libri Elucidarii, sermones et capitulo (*sic*) qui sequuntur.

In primis post librum Elucidarij . . . . f. 3

[Cent. xv, 26 or 27 lines to a page: headed, Que puer incipiet. hec deus expediet.]

Sermo sancti Anselmi Cantuariensis archiepiscopi Ad interioris hominis custodiam in quo sunt diuerse questiones [in the same hand] 58

Prologus beati Ieronimi presbiteri de natiuitate beate Marie virginis et de uita eiusdem uirginis dei genitricis Marie 62

[In the same hand: the text begins on f. 62 *b*, headed: Incipit vita sancte dei genitricis et virginis Marie secundum S. Jeronimum sexto Septembris. *Igitur beata et gloriosa.* Tischdf. *Evv. Apocr.* p. 113.]

[Additio de duobus miraculis. Post natiuitatem gloriosi domini nostri 67
A notice of the Assumption, of the death of S. John, of the death of Julian the Apostate, and of the story of Theophilus.

Nota quod Joseph non cognoscebat Mariam 68
The Virgin's face shone from the Conception to the Nativity, so that Joseph could not look upon her.

De etate marie . . . . 68 *b*
She was 14 at the Nativity, 63 at the Assumption.

De assumpcione. Two notes] . . . . 68 *b*

De incarnacione domini nostri Ihesu Christi Augustinus . . 69
Inter cetera et ad locum lege cum timore caute et secrete.

Vidi portam in domo domini clausam 69

Iesse pater est . . . . 69 *b*

De originali peccato . . . . 69 *b*
Dialogue between *discipulus* and *magister*.

De signis que uenerunt ante natiuitatem domini nostri Ihesu Christi et in tempore natiuitatis eius. *In augusti cesaris tempore* . . 72

[Two quatrains (*a*) on the reason why women are beautiful . . 72 *b*
(*b*) on the Fall.

Three lines on the signs of good wine . . . . 72 *b*

Three lines on long measure . . . . 72 *b*

Things to be observed by a dying Christian . . . . . . 73 *a*

Weights, measures, and coins of England . . . . . . 73 *a*

f. 73 *b* has only late notes.]

Ne tardas conuerti ad dominum (Liber Ricardi de Hampole de aedificatione spirituali *or* De emendatione peccatoris) 74

Contempnere mundum (part of the same tract) 76

Si uis perfectus esse 77

Vt homo ad honorem dei . . . . 78 *b*

Cum diabolus uiderit . . . . 81 *b*

Non dedignentur filii regis 82

Si in tribulacione vel temptacione fueris 84

Est autem meditacio bona de passione christi . . . . . . 84 *b*

Si cupis ad amorem dei peruenire . . . . 86 *b*

Per hos nouem gradus pretaxatos 87

Dulce lumen et delectabile 88

Contemplatio uel uita contemplatiua 92

Oleum effusum nomen tuum . . . . 95 *b*

Cum infeliciter florem (De incendio amoris) . . . . . . 100 *b*

Adolescentule dilexerunt te nimis . . . . 103 *b*

[At end: Explicit questio notabilis de spirituali edificacione componitur de Ricardi heremita de Hampole qui obiit anno domini M° · CCC° · XL° · IX° ·]

Decalogus est sermo breuis decem dei mandata continens . . . 108 *a*
A tract on the Decalogue and the plagues of Egypt.

Item racionem decalogi (on the same) . . . . 114 *b*

Quicunque vult confiteri Explicit summa confessionis Magistri Roberti de; (*sic*) . . . . 116 *b*

Sequitur de septem peccatis mortalibus exposicio secundum ordinem (followed by verses on confession) . . . . . . 125 *b*
Nota quod duplex est uita (followed by verses on the duties of a server at the altar, etc.) 127
Post peccatum Ade eodem expulso de paradiso 128
The Story of the Cross.
Mirabiliter oriri cepit sancta arbor . . . . 134 *b*
A continuation, concerning the death of Judas (see p. 75).
Septem sunt peticiones in oracione dominica 136
On the Lord's Prayer.
Nichil adeo venale quod non fiat mortale . . . . . . 137 *b*
Extracts on sin and fasting.
Paulus de penis inferni 138
Paulus apostolus interrogauit angelum domini quot essent pene in inferno. Cui ait angelus: Centum quadraginta quatuor milia (5 lines).
[Miscellaneous extracts] . . . . 138 *b*
Quod sola contricio non sufficit ad delendum peccatum sine confessione 139
An extract from 'Parisiensis' about Charles, K. of France, and S. Giles.
Terribile erit cum dominus dicet surgite mortui . . . . . 139 *b*
[Miscellaneous extracts] 140
Diabolus ludit cum peccatore . . . . 140 *b*
Nota quod ubi aliquis tenet pomum 141
Si percipis coruum nidificare 141
Tria genera hominum designantur per ovem . . . . . . 141 *b*
De vii vicijs.
Superbia stark, Inuidia cold, Ira pale, Accidia heuỳ, Auaricia not welle, Gula gr*oss* to behold, Luxuria stynkyng, etc.
The hand changes on f. 142.
Nemo vestimenta preciosa, and other extracts . . . . . . 142 *b*
Si uis corrigere delinquentem (an extract from Jerome) . . . 144 *b*
Abbathia de spiritu sancto (in another hand, 28 lines to a page) . 146
My dere breþeren and sistren[1].
De dieta et tonitruo duodecim mensium . . . . 172 *b*
Aleyn þe gode leche seiþ þath in þe mone of ianiuerie wyte wynes is gode.
Ypocrase de medisinis . . . . 173 *b*
Ipocras made þeise medicines for þe eueles in þe hed and for þe hed worke.
Many miscellaneous excerpts and several charms follow.
De expositione iiii^or^ partium anni per argumentum prophecie Iosep et filiorum suorum 183
The writing is smaller: the contents, a forecast of the year

[1] This tract, formerly attributed to Bishop Alcock, but at least a century older than his time, has been edited by the Rev. G. G. Perry for the E. Eng. Texts Soc., 1867 and 1889, *Religious Pieces*. This MS. is not used in that edition.

according to the day of the week on which Christmas Day falls.

Adam de octo partibus fuit factus 184

Also on the naming of Adam.

Tria sunt que vendicant hominem . . . . 184 *b*

De xii^cim^ causis que omni homini timende sunt . . . . 184 *b*

Qui abscondit scelera sua (from Proverbs) 185

Que auferunt venialia peccata . . . . 185 *b*

De significacione ecclesie . . . . 185 *b*

De significacione altaris 186

De diuite et lazaro . . . . 186 *b*

Here the old table stops.

Sacerdos debet esse vir sanctus (in another hand) 187

Dominus papa (erased) *Johannes xxij^us^* . . . . . . 187 *b*

Indulgences and extracts.

f. 187 *b* (wrongly numbered) has two late verses:

Dat Clemens hyemem, dat Petrus ver cathedratus.
Estuat Urbanus, autumnat Bartholomeus.

Part II. Cent. xii, xiii: 34 lines to a page.

Sermones de Sanctis 188

1. Prologue: Dilectissimis fratribus suis dilectissimus eorum frater....Postquam reuocatus sum a curia....He writes these sermons as a counterblast to profane literature. Quid enim tullio et apostolo? quid uirgilio et euangelio? quid petro cum mago? He is a Benedictine.
2. *De S. Joh. Baptista.* Hodie dilectissimi dies illuxit insignis 188
3. *In nat. app. Petri et Pauli.* Hodierna dies dilectissimi clara est 192 *b*
4. *De S. Maria Magdalena.* Hodie misericordia et veritas . 196
5. *De S. Petro.* Adolescentule dilexerunt te nimis . . . 199 *b*
6. *De S. Maria.* Hic totum decurrat ingenium . . . 201 *b*
7. *De cruce.* De uirga Iesse deuenimus ad uirgam crucis . . 207 *b*
8. *In dedicacione.* Post crucem post angelos post uirginem . 212

The hand changes to a larger and more regular one.

9. *De S. Victore.* Hic est ille magnus prouidentie oculus . . 214

...Ad manum est patris nostri Victoris sollempnitas, ad cuius sacratissimum si uera est antiquitatis fides cotidie residemus...

The author is therefore most likely a monk of S. Victor at Paris.

10. *In Natali omnium Sanctorum.* Hodie dies serenior arrisit uobis . . . . 215 *b*
11. *De S. Martino.* Nobilis ille confessor . . . . . . 217 *b*
12. *De S. Andrea.* Et quietum studium 220
13. *De S. Nicholao.* Nicholaus iste meus immo uester . . 221
14. *De S. Maria.* Exultate fratres in domino . . . . . 222 *b*
15. *In Nat. Domini.* Tandem de mari ad portum 225
16. O quam pulcra . . . . 227 *b*
17. *De S. Benedicto.* Uenite ad me omnes qui laboratis . . 228
18. Induite uos armatura dei 229

19. *De S. Maria.* Vidi speciosam sicut columbam . . . 230
20. (*De angelis.*) Circa rerum cardinem uersamur . . . 231 *b*
21. Narrat diuina hystoria quod Tobyas 235
22. De Samsone quomodo deceptus sit . . . . . . 235 *b*

There are no more titles for a considerable time, and the sermons become mere paragraphs of a few lines each.

The hand changes after quire vii at f. 244: 37 lines to a page.

In pasca. Cum transisset sabbatum . . . . . . 249 *b*

Sermo in ieiunio. Gubernator prudens 258

f. 259 *b* is blank. On f. 260 the hand changes again to double columns of 33 lines each.

In assumptione S. Marie. Signum magnum apparuit . . 260

On 261 *b* is another change of hand continued to the end: irregular writing of 29 lines to a page follows.

Sibilabit dominus musce . . . . 261 *b*

Fecit rex Salomon tronum 262

Immisit dominus somnum in Adam 263

Short sermons follow: the last is longer:

Christus assistens pontifex . . . . 266 *b*

On 267 *b* is a late quatrain with English glosses.

The following is a copy of such parts of the will (see p. 70) as I could read.

go Dionis pos ita condo testamentum meum

in ecclesia iuxta corpus

de oli It' cuilibet aquario dicte ecclesie vj d It' sacerdoti parochiali vj d

keston It' lego Domino Will^{mo} Bernard si voluerit celebrare in ecclesia

ey quondam patris mei centum s. si predictus Will^{s} noluerit vel inmediate mor

filiol It. pauperibus egentibus in sex villis propinquantibus ville de W

t' priori vj s viij d et cuilibet canonico domus xii d It' fratri

cistam It. agneti Addurbery moniali de stevle domina mais'

er meam crateram de argento cum coopertorio et sex cocliaria argentea

teram argent coopertorio It. quatuor ordinibus religiosorum de Northamton

Worsted duo paria lintheam*inum* et duabus W^{h}yialiss It. domino Will^{mo} Red.

s. It. hulkote vj s viij d. Jt. cuilibet filio meo de sacro fonte ,

ry x uxori Symonis Ardyss j Note cum couerclio It. Alicie J

me Northamtone detur pauperibus ut predixi domino Will^{mo} Bern

It. fu rnaby vj s viij d Jt. cuilibet seruienti filii mei vt

I^{t} Eliz sorori mee vnam togam russetam penulatam cum greye It.

grum. It. Johanni Peronell vnam marcam. It. Thome fil. Will^{i} Debo

d vj d xij d It. Stephano Coppole vj d It. Johanne Wa

mentum perficiendum constituo executores meos Joh^{m} Olney filium

non nent et disponant prout saluti anime mee magis viderint prope

It. lego Elizabet vnum paruum cauderum et vnum chawfer

e arg got filie dys ij s. It. Roberto Smyth

Piper eius ij s It. Joh. Taylor et vxori eius ij s It. Thom

yn eius ij s Jt. Andree kentoe xij d It. Bernardo

It. sc vj s viij d

f. 134 *b*

Mirabiliter oriri cepit sancta arbor de tribus uirgulis composita. Prima erat Cip*res*sina alia Cedrina et Pini speciem habuit tertia. Cypressus patrem Cedrus filium Pinus spiritum sanctum significat de quibus facta est christi (crux) adoranda. Et mirabilius in terra stetit usque ad tempus Dauid regis nichil crescens nec uiriditatem nec foliorum teneritudinem perdens set per omnia sic permansit sicut primo Moisi apparuit donec sanctus Dauid meruit illam de loco transferre et in orto suo reponere. Jbi ·u· erat illa crescens ut xxx[ta] annis efficeretur arbor grandis; hec inter omnes arbor uua nobilis. Ex illis tribus uirgulis creuit quas dei amicus Moyses a sompno excitatus circa se reperit exortas per tres noctes continuas quas dei amicus deo dilectus Dauyd ad Ierusalem detulit: ibi in viridario suo collocatus per annos xxx[ta] coluit. et unoquoque anno in illarum summitate unum argenteum circulum innexuit. Et reliquos inferius innexos dilatauit ut arbor dilataretur in grossum et extenderetur in longum. ille uirgule continuatam habentes uiriditatem in unam simil*em* concreuerunt arborem. Que arbor mire suauitatis erat in estate et ẏeme immarcescibiles fr*on*[135]dium flores protulit. Tempore peracto laudabilis arbor cedris libani omnibus sublimior iussu regis Salamonis succisa est ad edificacionem templi et cum nullo modo coaptari poterit et coequari, in crucifixionem tantummodo corporis Christi digna fuit coaptari in qua uita mundi pependit, in qua Christus triumphauit. Et xxx[ta] aureos circulos in templo suspensos uesani acceperunt Iudei et dederunt infelici Iude pro tradicione domini nostri ut esset ueraciter impletum quod dicitur per prophetam: Apprehenderunt mercedem xxx[ta] argenteis quos appreciatus (sum) ab eis. Et in passione domini secundum mathei *com*posicionem de eodem infelici Iuda scriptum est quod adiret principes sacerdotum et inquireret ab eis precium nostri saluatoris ita inquiens. Quid uultis mihi dare et ego eum uobis tradam. At illi constituerunt ei xxx[ta] argenteos, illos uidelicet predictos circulos qui templo pendebant, quos communiter possidebant et quos infelix Iudas accepit pro tradicione domini nostri. Et uendito Ihesu Christo rediit ad domum suam et retulit matri sue per ordinem quomodo tradidit dominum Audiens autem eius mater quod ab eo traditus esset in furorem conversa est et lacrimata est dicens. Heu me miseram qui te genui celeratum filium. Quid tibi et iusto illi? Quare infelix iustum et sanctum tradere uoluisti. Nunc ergo absque dubitacione omnes maledicciones implebuntur in te <que> [135 *b*] per prophetam ita sunt scripte ffiant filii eius orphani et uxor eius uidua et cetera que secuntur in illo psalmo. Non enim ut estimas filium hominis tradidisti sed unigenitum dei filium et ecce a te sanguis eius exquisitus et tu reus mortis eius extiteris. vere de illo propheta dicit Filius hominis uadit sicut scriptum est de eo: ue illi per quem traditus fuerit. Nunc ergo fili doloris mei quid acturus quid dicturus eris dum ueritatis prophetam a mortuis resurrexisse cognoueris? Ad uocem igitur lacrimose matris in iracundiam prouocatus Iudas respexit ad focum uiditque super eum ollam feruentem stantem et in ea semicoctum gallum iacentem, clamauitque ad matrem suam. Quomodo in tantum deuenisti errorem ut illum amentem dicas fuisse prophetam atque a mortuis aliquem resurrecturum? Ego autem per maximum affirmo iuramentum quod de ista poterit olla facilius hic depilatus exire gallus quam resurgere a mortuis ille crucifixus. Hec dum infelix ganniret et ad modum wlpis clamaret Iudas, semicoctus gallus effectus est rediuiuus et protinus de feruenti olla exiliens apparuit pulcherimus pennisque et plumis restitutus et uolauit super tecta domus ibique diu mansit ouans et gaudens quasi pronunciaret tempus resurrectionis christi. Affirmat ergo edi[136]cio grecorum hunc eundem extitisse gallum qui eadem nocte cum cantando Petrum arguit negantem. super quem lacrimantem dominus continuo respexit. Hoc autem signo infelix Iudas territus abiit ad locum ubi passus est Christus: uidensque illum esse dampnatum proiecit in templo argenteos unde prius fuerunt abstracti fuerunt a Iudeis et abiens laqueo se suspendit. Sicut pater suus antequam ipsum procreauit diuinauit. Erat enim pater eius astrologus qui eadem nocte in qua genitus fuerat Iudas respexit planetas et uidit et ita intimauit uxori sue quod siquis eadem hora noctis generaret filium quod ille filius patrem proprium occideret et dominum suum detraheret et se ultimo laqueo suspenderet. Quod factum est sicut prophetauit. Nam statim pater predicti infelicis Iude accessit ad uxorem suam nec se potuit abstinere et filium iniquitatis procreauit. Qui patrem proprium submersit dominum suum fefellit laqueo se suspendit et sic patet eius origo et eius ffinis.

f. 179 *b*. *A charm • iij • tymes sayde ouere a wounde.*

Ibant tres boni fratres ad montem oliueti bonas herbas querentes omnia wlnera sanantes. obuiauerunt domino Ihesu Christo: quo tenditis tres boni fratres: Domine ad montem oliueti bonas herbas querentes omnia uulnera sanantes Reuertimini tres boni fratres et accipietis olium oliue et lanam bidentis et ponetis super wlnera et coniuretis uulnera per quinque plagas domini noster Ihesu Christi et per mamillas que lactauerunt Christum quod non doleat neque ranclat nec fetescat plusquam fecerunt wlnera domini nostri J. C. quando suspensus erat in cruce sed sanetur a profundo sicut wlnus quod longeus fecit in dextro latere Christi. In nomine etc. Amen.

47. Q. D. 6.

NEW TESTAMENT IN ENGLISH.

Vellum, $6\frac{1}{2} \times 4\frac{5}{8}$, ff. 394, double columns of 30 lines. Cent. xiv or early xv.

Collation: i^{10} ii^{10} iii^{14} ‖ a^8–r^8 ꝛ^8 ſ^8 s^8 t^8 u^8 v^8 w^8 x^8 y^8 þ^8 z^8 ꝫ^8 &^{8} 9^8 ÷^{8} A^8–C^8 D^8 (wants 5) E^8–N^8 O^2 (2 blank, gone).

Binding: of xviith or xviiith cent.

The hand is exceedingly fine and clear, and the ornamental work—not large in quantity—is excellent in quality.

The lost leaf, D 5, contained the end of 1 John, 2 John, and beginning of 3 John.

On f. ii 9 *b* is this note:

M. d. y[t] aftre y[e] deathe off Mrs Cottrell she beyinge y[e] owner yeroff hathe gyuen y[is] same to Edmunde Gryndall fellow off pembroake hall in Cambryge. M.

A fine hand of cent. xvi, xvii has added:

Hic liber postmodum devenit in manus cuiusdam David moris alias Hanmer, in artibus magistri, dum in domo honoratissimi herois domini Gulielmi Cecilii filium eius natu maximum institueret: unde post multos exantlatos labores in ulteriorem Salopiensis agri partem secessit, et scholae Oswaldiensis moderato evasit, quam per 30 aut eo plus annos faeliciter rexit. Cuius filius unicus Johannes moris alias Hanmer, paternis virtutibus exornatus, huius quem tenes libri copiam mihi facere voluit: vt ex subsequentibus eius ad me literis colligere possis

Dilectissimo suo Edvardo Hughes Cantabrigiae Collegii Ihesu socio Johannes Hanmerus Suenianus Salopiensis S. D.

The writer excuses himself for having left Hughes's letter so long unanswered, on the ground that for 12 years he had been studying Law, and had forgotten his Latin. He then makes the offer of this MS., which he had inherited from his father, once Hughes's tutor; the letter is dated E Tuguriolo nostro Sueniae iuxta Oswestriam Salopiae Calend. Februarii 1594.

Hughes continues:

Atqui ut hunc publici iuris facerem et huic sedi literariae dedicarem, quem mihi ad priuatum studiorum usum dedit Hanmerus meus, impulit imprimis pietas mea in hanc nutricem meam, cui me meaque omnia debere profiteor ingenue: necnon imperauit publicae utilitatis ratio, quae (me iudice) non uult ut tanti pretii gemma intra priuati cuiusquam demortui scrinia tineis corroderetur. Gratis ergo fruatur posteritas Iesuana hoc qualicunque munusculo, post tot annorum lustra Cantabrigiæ quasi postliminio reuocato.

Cui ex animo dat consecratque Edwardus Hughes quondam huius Collegii Socius.

On the top of the first page is the name Rd. Murkeeston. (? t)

Contents:

1. Here bigynneþ a table of þe newe testament. þese ben þe maters of þe gospel of mathew . . . . f. i 1
2. Here bigynneþ a rule þat telliþ in whiche chapitris of þe bible ȝe mai fynde þe lessouns pistlis and gospellis þ[t] ben red in þe chirche at þe ȝeer aftir þe vss of salisbirie, markid wiþ lettris of þe abc. at þe bigynnynge of þe chapitris twoward þe myddil or eende af*ter* þe ordre as þe lettris stonden in þe abc. ffirst ben sett sondaies and ferials togidere. And aftir þat þe sanctorum boþe þe propre and comyn togidere of al þe ȝeer. ffirst is writen a clause of þe bigynnynge þerof: and a clause of þe eendynge þerof also ffor it bigynneþ at þe lettris of the abc. and endiþ at twei strikis in þe margyn.
   1. Sondai in aduent } romans xiii *d* we knowen *ende* lord ihu crist // m[t] xxi *a* whanne ihc *ende* in hiȝe þingis //
3. The text of the New Testament, with Prologues. Evv., Paul., Act., Cath., Apoc.
4. Here eendiþ þe apocalips of Jon þe laste book of þe newe testament: and bigynneþ þe lessouns and pistlis of þe olde testament þ[t] ben red in þe chirche bi al þe ȝeere . . . f. G 4 *b*

48. Q. D. 7.

BOETHIUS.

Vellum, 7 × 5, ff. 354, 27 and 29 lines to the page. Cent. xiii, xv.

Binding: white skin over boards: has had two clasps. Given by Mr Man.

Collation: a^8 b^8 c^{10} (wants 6) d^{12} (wants 11) e^{12} f^8 || g^{16} (wants 11, 16 blank) || h^{12} i^{10} (wants 5, 10 blank) || k^{12}–z^{12} aa^{12}–gg^{12}.

Provenance: Durham: the name has been cut off, but the following inscription is left on the 4th fly-leaf at the beginning, in a hand resembling that of the Durham inscriptions in general:

O. Quinque libri boecij de consolacione philosophie cum tabula.
ii. Exposicio super quinque libros predictos satis certe notabilis.

I do not find it in *Catt. Vett.*

Contents:

1. Boethius de consolatione philosophie, cent. xiii . . . f. 1
   With many marginal and interlinear glosses.
   f. 27 is of xvth cent. inserted in the 3rd piece of Book v. (on f. 56 *b* the older hand leaves off and one of xvth cent. continues). The text ends on f. 66: ff. 66 *b*–70 *b* are blank.
2. Table to the above, of cent. xvi.
   A good border of English work, gold, blue, green, pink, orange, on f. 71.
   The table ends on 86 *a*: 86 *b*–90 *b* are blank.
3. Commentary (by Nicolas Trivet) on the *De Consolatione* . 91
   Explanacionem librorum boecij de cons. phil. aggressurus.
   Begins with an account of Boethius, drawn apparently from Freculphus.
   There is a good border on f. 91 and a plainer one at the beginning of each book of the Commentary: these borders are of the same character as that on f. 71.
   Diagrams occur occasionally in the Commentary.

49. Q. G. 1.

SELECTA EX AUGUSTINO.

Vellum, 10⅝ × 7, ff. 147, 36 lines to a page. Cent. xii.

Collation: i^8–xii^8 xiii^4 (wants 4, a blank leaf) a^8–e^8 f^{10} (wants 1: 10 is a blank leaf attached to the cover).

The binding is the original boards, covered with white vellum and formerly fastened by two straps and pins, of which the lower one remains. There is a chain-mark on the middle of the lower edge of the 1st cover. It is no. 3 in James's *Ecloga Cantabrigiensis* (1600), p. 137.

Provenance. On the inside of the first cover is a xvth cent. table of contents:

Contenta huius libri sunt hec:

1. Aurelius Augustinus doctor egregius super genesim ad literam in • 12 • libris.
2. Aug. de gratia noui testamenti.
3. Aug[i] prologus ex primo libro Retractationum.
4. Aug. de vtilitate credendi.
5. Aug. de laude karitatis.
6. Omnis diuina scriptura.

In another hand below:

Liber m. Johannis gunthorp' decani Wellensis emptus London xx decembris a[o] xpi 1484[to] pro quindecim solidis solutis.

The 2nd leaf begins *linguarum diuersitas.*

The binding and the handwriting of the table of contents, as well as the folio-numbering, recall very strongly the Bury MSS., but there is no press-mark. This may have been on one of two fly-leaves lost at the beginning.

There are traces of a title in Lombardic letters along the back: the handwriting of the table of contents is, I think, that of the Librarian of Bury in cent. xv[1].

Contents:

1. Augustinus super Genesim ad literam libri xii . . . . . f. 1 *a*
   In single lines, 40 to the page, in a fine hand. The quires are marked in Roman figures i–xii. It has suffered from damp in the middle; f. 99 *b* is blank. An initial has been cut out of f. 1. The headings are in red and green capitals.
2. Augustinus de gratia noui testamenti 100
   In double columns of 36 lines each: an initial on f. 100 has been cut out.
3. Prologus ex libro primo retractatus S. Augustini . . . . 124 *aa*
4. Liber S. Augustini ad Honoratum de utilitate credendi . . 125 *ba*
5. Sermo S. Augustini de laude karitatis.
   Divinarum scripturarum multiplicem . . . . . . 141 *bb*
6. A tract without title, in paler ink.
   (O)mnis diuina scriptura circa triplicem intellectum . . . 143 *aa*
   Gregory is quoted. Ends imperfectly: Heliseus domini salus interpretatur.
   ff. 146, 147 are in single columns, 32 lines to the page.
   On the inside of the cover is an unfinished outline of a bearded man (Christ) xii–xiiith cent. and the price, written in xvth cent. precium xv s.

See the present writer's Essays *On the Abbey of S. Edmund at Bury*, pp. 3, 46.

50. Q. G. 2.

YSAIAS, TOBIT, RUTH, GLOSATI.

Vellum, $9\frac{7}{8} \times 6\frac{1}{8}$, ff. 134, 15 lines of text on most pages. Cent. xii, xiii. Two volumes in one.

Binding: the original boards, covered with brown leather.

Collation: i^8–xiiii^8 xv^4 ‖ a^{12} b^6: 134 leaves.

Contents:

The gloss on Tobit and Ruth is in a larger and coarser hand, not much later than that on Isaiah.

Provenance: Durham. There is a xvth cent. press-mark: Є (in black letter) and an erased number on the cover: also a xvth century title 'ysaias glosatus et tobias glosatus': the Є alone occurs on f. 1 *a*. See *Catt. Vett.* 15, E. Ysaias et Thobias glo. ii fo., "wlnus et L." The volume was presented to the College by Mr Man, Fellow, Jan. 21, 1685.

Parts of two leaves from a large xiiith cent. Missal in double columns are attached to the covers: that at the end contains the Gospel of the Paralytic (Lc. v. 18), the collect *Sacrificia domine tuis oblata conspectibus*, the antiphon *Spiritus ubi uult spirat alleluia*, post-communion *Sumpsimus domini sacri dona misterii humiliter deprecantes.* Last line a rubric: *Sabbato si ieiunium non fuerit.* There is a good rough initial to the gloss on Isaiah, f. 1 *a*.

51. Q. G. 3.

SPECULUM CHRISTIANI.

Vellum, $9 \times 5\frac{1}{2}$, ff. 42, 30 lines to a page. Cent. xv.

Coarse vellum, somewhat soiled.

Collation: a^{10}–d^{10} e^2: 42 leaves.

The book was printed by W. de Machlinia in 1484 (?). It contains a good deal of English. A version of the Ten Commandments was printed from this MS. by Wright and Halliwell in *Reliquiae Antiquae.* The author is said by Tanner to have been John Watton.

The MS. was presented to the College by Mr Man, Jan. (21) 1685. The binding is modern.

52. Q. G. 4.

IVONIS CARNOTENSIS ET ALIORUM SERMONES, ETC.

Vellum, $8\frac{5}{8} \times 5$, ff 45, 36 and 37; 32 lines to a page: three volumes bound in one. Cent. xii. Finely written.

Given to the College by Mr Man, Jan. 21, 1685.

Collation: a^8–c^8 d^6 || e^8 || f^8 (wants 1, blank): 45 leaves.

Contents:

I. 1. Ivonis Carnotensis Episcopi 7 Sermones.

1.	Corruptum peccatis	f. 1 *a*
2.	De aduentu domini. Quoniam presentium	3 *b*
3.	De natiuitate domini Ihesu Christi. In diuine miserationis	5 *a*
4.	De circumcisione domini. Dominici natalis hodie	6 *b*
5.	De epiphania domini. Hunc epýphaniorum diem	7 *b*
6.	De purificatione marie. Consuetudo ecclesiastica	8 *b*
7.	De septuagesima. Scientes dilectissimi	9 *b*
8.	De capite ieiunij. Hodie mater ecclesia	11 *a*
9.	De quadragesima. Audiuit fraternitas	12 *a*
10.	De adnuntiatione S. Marie. Gaudeamus in domino	13 *a*
11.	In ramis palmarum. Qui wlt hominem	15 *a*
12.	In cena domini. Optatus nobis	16 *a*
13.	De pascha. Cum cetere festiuitates	16 *b*
14.	De ascensione domini. Hodie fratres uictoria	17 *b*
15.	De pentecosten. Dies Pentecostes sacratus	18 *a*

2. Liber B. Augustini de uita christiana ad sororem suam uiduam 20 *a*
A xviith cent. note here says: Fastidij Britanni, ut nuper probavit Lucas Holstenius et edidit Romae 1663, vide Cavei Hist. litter. de Fastidio, vide Caveum p. 310 1 vol. Fastidius is mentioned by Gennadius *de Vir. Illustr.* 56. The book is printed in Galland, ix. 481–489. The opening words in the MS. are Et ego peccator et ultimus insipientiorque ceteris.
f. 30 is blank.

II. 3. A tract without title.
Exceptiones ecclesiasticarum regularum, partim ex epistolis romanorum pontificum . . . . 31 *a*
f. 38 is blank.

III. 4. Sermo B. Augustini ep. de decem preceptis legis et de decem plagis egyptiorum . . . . 39 *a*

5. Libellus de iiii^or uirtutibus id est prudentia fortitudine temperantia et iustitia martini episcopi ad mironem regem. This tract is often attributed to Seneca: see Lightfoot's *Philippians*, p. 331 . . . . 41 *a*
ff. 44 *b*, 45 are blank.

The volume is bound in a leaf of a folio Psalter, xiii–xiv cent., in double columns, showing part of Ps. cxviii. (cxix.) *Mirabilia testimonia—Clamaui in toto corde meo.* At each end are two leaves of a smaller Psalter (cent. xiii) of 24 lines to a page. The leaves at the beginning are nos. 3 and 5 of a quire, those at the end are 1 and 8 of the same quire. More leaves will be found in Q. G. 5, etc. Those in this volume contain parts of Pss. (1) lxi.–lxiii.; (3) lxv., lxvi.; (5) lxviii.; (8) lxix., lxx.

On f. 38 *b* is a faint scribble (xvth cent.):

Os dauy harpe a lay you sorps al to lang.

There are tags from a MS. of cent. xiii, xiv.

53. Q. G. 5.

Ivonis Carnotensis Epistolae.

Vellum, 8½ × 4⅝, ff. 36; 37, 30, 36 lines to a page. Cent. xii. Well written.

Given to the College by Mr Man, Jan. 21, 1685.

Collation: a^8 b^{12} c^8 d^8.

Contents:

44. To Gaufridus of Beauvais.
45. To Pope Urban.
46. To Manegoldus.
47. To Roszelinus.
48. To the Nuns in Dumensi monasterio.
49. To Philip King of France.
50. To Rainaldus of Rheims.
51. To Philip.
52. To Robert. 53. To Thomas of York. 54. To Haimeric.

At the beginning are two leaves from the same Psalter, and the same quire of it, as in the last MS. They are leaves 2 and 7 of the quire, and contain parts of Pss. lxiii., lxiv. and lxviii., lxix.

54. Q. G. 6.

THOMAS DE ENTE, ETC.

Vellum, $8\frac{1}{2} \times 5\frac{1}{4}$, ff. 276, in varying numbers of lines to a page. Cent. xiii–xv.

Given by Mr Man, Jan. 21, 1685.

Collation: a^2 b^{14} (wants 13) c^{12} d^{12} e^{12} f^{12} g^{12} h^{12} i^{12} k^{12} l^{12} m^{10} n^{12} o^{12} p^4 q^{10} r^{12} (wants 11, 12) ‖ s^{10} t^{12} u^{14} (wants 9–14) ‖ v^{12} w^{12} x^{12} ‖ y^{12} z^{12} aa^6 (wants 6): 276 leaves.

Provenance: Durham. On f. 15 *b* is the title:

Breuiloquium de virtutibus antiquorum principum ac philosophorum 2° fo. quod habebat.

Then in another hand:

Iste liber assignatur Nono (nouo?) Armariolo in claustro Dunelmensis Ecclesie per venerabilem Patrem Magistrum Johannem Auklande priorem eiusdem Ecclesie.

Both these inscriptions are of cent. xv.

Contents:

On f. 2 *b* is a table of contents: the top of the leaf is cut off.

1. Tractatus de ente et essencia (by Thomas Aquinas) . . . f. 1
2. Breuiloquium de virtutibus antiquorum principum et philosophorum (by Bonaventura) 16
3. Diuersa themata predicatoribus proficua 34
   Convertimini ad me in toto corde uestro. A collection of 23 sermons, with *Exempla*, *Applicationes* etc.
   ff. 65–69 are left blank for an Index, which is not finished.
4. Moralitates super ysaiam prophetam 70
   Beatus qui custodit uerba prophetie huius.

5. Libri 19 de animalibus et eorum proprietatibus moribus hominum applicatis . . . . 94 *b*
Omnia secundum apostolum inuisibilia dei per ea que facta sunt intellecta conspiciuntur.
f. 159 *b* is blank.

6. Declamaciones senece et aliorum philosophorum dicta moralizata.
A table on f. 160 *a*. Text . . . . 160 *b*
1. *De redempcione generis humani.* (F)ertur ut repperi in quadam veteri historia quendam Imperatorem habuisse filiam.
2. *De misericordia dei ad nos.* Seneca li° 1° declamacionum declamacione 5ta Rapta raptoris morte aut nupcias petat.

7. De 7 mortalibus (peccatis et) eorum effectibus et incomodis et hi bis continetur cum versibus in margine . . . 182
Another hand.
Superbia est elacio viciosa.

8. Sermones quidam . . . . 195 *b*

9. De quinque septenis in sacra scriptura inuentis . . . 238
Quinque septena in sacra scriptura inueni que volo si possum puris enumerando ab inuicem distinguere.
ff. 245–247 blank.

10. De 7 mortalibus peccatis ut supra 248
The same tract as no. 7 in another hand.

11. Alie notule morales cum aliis . . . . 261 *b*
P. si vtique est fructus iusto? utique est, vnde ẏsa. Dicite iusto quoniam bene erit ei.
A number of miscellaneous notes on words and texts.

12. ff. 273–276 are in a different hand and contain sermons (apparently six) in a bad hand.
In disciplina perseuerate tanquam filiis se offert dominus.

55. Q. G. 7.

ORDINALE PRAEMONSTRATENSIUM.

Paper, 8 × 5½, ff. 143, 30 lines to a page. Cent. xv (late).

Binding: brown stamped leather over wooden boards, formerly fastened with strap and pin. There are 3 stamps used—(1) triangular with a trefoil flower or leaf, (2) lozenge-shaped, with a fleur-de-lys, (3) square with a Greek cross fleury. They are scattered quite irregularly over the cover, 20 on one side and 23 on the other. Given by Mr Man.

Collation: a^{12}–e^{12} f^{10} g^{12} h^{14} i^{12} k^{12} l^{14} (2 cancelled) m^{12} (9 is two leaves pasted together).

Provenance. On f. 1 is written:

Iste liber constat Johanni Tanfyld canonici de skyrpynes[1].

Two parchment fly-leaves at either end are cut from a vellum roll which had been taken round to various monasteries to solicit their prayers for the soul of William Yorke, abbot of the house to which the book belonged. The first entry is:

A. (1) Titulus monasterii Beate Marie...(? Ebor.) | Ordinis Sancti Benedicti. Anima (Dom)ni Willelmi Zorke Abbatis Et Anime | (omnium) | ffidelium Defunctorum per misericordiam dei In p(ace requi)|escant. Amen.

Vestris Nostra Damus pro nostris uestra (rogamus).

(2) Titulus monasterii B. Marie de Elsham ord. S. Augustini = Ellesham in Lincolnshire.

(3) Titulus mon. B. M. de Thornton ord. S. Augustini linc. dioc. (Thorneton-on-Humber or Thornton Curteis.)

(4) Tit. mon. B. M. sanctique marcialis.. de Neuhous ord. premonstr. linc. dioc. (Newhouse.)

(5) Tit. mon. beatorum Augustini et Olaui de Walhow, ord. S. Aug. linc. dioc. (Wellow, near Grimsby.)

(6) Tit. monast. b. M. de Cothome. (Cotham in Lincoln, Cistercian nuns.)

Verso. (This follows fragment C.)

B. (1) Tit. ecclesie Cath. b. Marie de Coventr. ord. S. Bened.

(2) Tit. mon. b. M. de Cumba ord. Cist. Covent. et Lych. dioc. (Combe in Warwick.)

(3) Tit. ordinis fratrum heremitarum S. Aug. Laycystrie. (? Priory of S. Katherine in Leicester.)

(4) Tit. fratrum ord. predicatorum conuentus Leycystrie. (Black Friars at Leicester.)

(5) Tit. monast. B. M. de pratis Leycestrie ord. S. Aug. linc. dioc. (S. Mary Pré at Leicester.)

(6) Tit. mon. B. M. de Vluescroft. ord. S. Aug.: Charley and Ulvescroft in Charnwood Forest.

(7) Tit. mon. (B. M.) de Garadon ord. Cist. Lincoln. dioc. (Gerondon in Leicestershire.)

(8) Tit. mon. de gracedea (?) lincoln. dioc. (Grace Dieu in Leicestershire?)

(9) Tit. mon. de langeley. (O. S. B. nuns, Langley in Leicestershire.)

(10) Tit. mon. de Croxton. (Praemonstr., Leicestershire.)

At the end of the volume is another piece of the roll.

Recto:

C. (1) Tit. fratrum predicatorum Wygornie. (Black Friars.)

(2) Tit. frat. minorum Wygornie. (Grey Friars.)

(3) Tit. monast. B. M. de Bordesley ord. Cist. Wigorn. dioc.

[1] I can find no Praemonstratensian house to suit this name: it may refer to the Hospital of Shireburn near Durham, which was a lazar-house and supported several priests.

(4) Tit. fr. ord. predicatorum Warwycie.

(5) Tit. mon. B. M. de Kenillworth ord. S. Aug. Couentr. et lich. dioc.

(6) Tit. mon. B. M. de Stonleya ord. Cist. Couentr. et lich. dioc. (Stanley-in-Arden.)

(7) Tit. fr. minorum Couentrie.

(8) Tit. domus S. Anne ord. Cart. prope Couentr. (Charterhouse at Coventry.)

Verso:

D. (1) Tit. mon. S. Agathe virg. et mart. iuxta Richmond ord. ... Ebor. dioc. (Praemonstratensian.)

(2) Tit. ord. frat. minorum Richmond.

(3) Tit. mon. B. M. de Couerham ord. Premonstr. Ebor. dioc. (Corham, near Richmond.)

(4) Tit. mon. B. M. de Joreualle ord. Cist. Ebor. dioc. (Jervaux.)

(5) Titulus ffr. (*sic*).

Frater Robartus minister domus S. Robarti iuxta Knaresburgh ordinis... (Trinitarians.)

(6) Tit. mon. B. M. de Nu*n*mownkton ord. premonstr. Ebor. dioc. (? Nun Monkton; but in Tanner this is a Benedictine nunnery.)

(7) Tit. ord. fr. minorum Ebor.

(8) Tit. fr. heremitarum ord. S. Aug. Ebor.

(9) Tit. fr. ord. Carmelitarum B. M. Ebor.

(10) Tit. ord. fr. predicatorum Ebor.

(11) Tit. mon. S. Trinitat. Ebor. ord. S. Benedicti. (Cell to Marmoutier.) Fragment A follows on this.

Rolls of this kind have been printed by the Surtees Society, e.g. the *Obituary Roll of Ebchester and Burnby.*

Contents:

An Ordinal, or Pie. The Preface runs as follows:

Regula de omnibus historiis inchoandis et de omnibus commemoracionibus faciendis per totum annum, tractata de ordinali premonstratensis ordinis per septem litteras kalendarii, et quilibet littera per se diuiditur in sex partes. Et hoc propter festa mobilia et annos bisextiles. Ideo in primis sciatis que sit littera dominicalis in anno iam presenti, deinde numerum per quem luna currit in eodem anno. Quibus cognitis intrate in regulam sequentem et querite eandem litteram dominicalem quousque inueneritis predictum numerum lunarem et predictam litteram dominicalem simul stantes. Quibus inuentis operamini cum eadem littera per totum annum iam presentem.

56. Q. G. 8.

LYDGATE, ETC.

Vellum, $8\frac{1}{2} \times 6\frac{1}{2}$, ff. 92, 32 lines to a page. English. Cent. xv. Presented by Mr Man.

Collation: A^6–P^6 Q^4 (wants 3, 4): 92 leaves.

Mr W. Aldis Wright, Vice-Master of Trinity College, is the author of the appended table of contents.

Contents:

Lydgate's Testament, printed from another MS. in Lydgate's *Minor Poems*, p. 232 (Percy Society).

1. O how holsom and glad is þe memorye . . . . . . f. 1 *a*

...

With *Ihū mercy kneling* on my *knee*.

Testamentum in nomine Jhu.

(T)he *yeres* passid of my *tender youth* . . . . . . 6 *a*

2. *Quis dabit capiti meo fontem lacrimarum* . . . . . 19 *b*

(W)ho shall yeue vnto *myn hede* a well.

...

That fore þ*er*e loue was nailed to a tre.

3. *Consulo quisquis eris qui pacis federa queris* . . . . . 22 *b*

Consonus esto lupis cum quibus esse cupis.

(I) counçail *what so* euere þou be.

...

To his plesaunce to othir his language.

Printed in Lydgate's *Minor Poems*, p. 173 (Percy Soc. ed. Halliwell) and in Furnivall's *Political, Religious and Love Poems*, p. 25 (E. E. T. S.) from other MSS.

4. *All stant in chaunge like a mydsomer Rose* . . . . . 25 *a*

Let no man bost of Ronnyng nor vertue.

...

Of whos v wound*es* prynte in youre herte a Rose.

Printed from this MS. in Lydgate's *Minor Poems*, p. 22.

5. Off god and kynde p*ro*cedith all beaute . . . . . . 27 *b*

...

By exsaumple of hir youre hornys cast away.

Printed in Halliwell and Wright's *Reliquiae Antiquae*, I. p. 79, and in *Minor Poems*, p. 46, from other MSS.

6. Towarde the eende of frosty Januarie . . . . . . 29 *a*

...

Looke welle youre myrrours and deme noon other night.

Printed in *Minor Poems*, p. 156, from another MS.

7. The worlde so wide the eyre so remevable . . . . . 33 *a*

...

Toward þat life where ioy is ay lastyng.

Printed in *Minor Poems*, p. 193, from another MS.

8. As of hony men gadre out swetnes . . . . 36 *a*

...

With hym to dwell aboue þe sterrys clere.

Printed in *Minor Poems*, p. 216, from another MS.

9. *Pax.*

Mercye and truth met on a high mountayn . . . . . 37 *b*

...

For vs to come to everlastyng pees.
Another MS. in Trin. Coll. Camb. R. 3. 21.

10. *Misericordias domini in eternum cantabo* . . . . . 41 *a*
All goostly songes and ympnes þat be sunge.
. . .
Eternally þi mercies þei do syng.
Another MS. in Trin. Coll. Camb. R. 3. 21.

11. *Incipit doctrina sana* . . . . 44 *a*
Who will be hole and kepe hym fro sekenes.
. . .
To all indifferent richest dietarie.
Printed in *Minor Poems*, p. 66 (except the stanzas 1–4) from another MS.

12. *Incipit tractatus de Regibus anglie post conquestum* . . 46 *a*
This myghty Willam duke of Normandye.
. . .
Longe to reioyssh and Regne here in his right.
This copy ends with Henry VI. Two other copies ending with Edward IV. are in MS. Trin. Coll. Camb. R. 3. 21.

13. *Incipit Pater noster* . . . . 47 *b*
A twine drede and tremblyng Reverence.
. . .
By goodly fauoure to correl of þeire grace.

14. *Incipiunt quindecim gaudia beate marie* . . . . . . 53 *a*
A twene mydnyght and þe fressh morowe g*ra*ye.
. . .
As hereto forre is shewid þe maner.
[Quindecim dolores beatae Mariae] . . . . . . 55 *b*
Without title: written as a continuation of the preceding.
As ye haue herde accomplysshid þe gladnes.
. . .
Where þu failest þat men shall þe correcte.

15. *De profundis clamaui* . . . . 58 *a*
Hauyng a conceyte in my symple wite.
. . .
At his chirch to hyng it on the wall.
Written in Lydgate's old age at the command of W. C., see last stanza.

16. *Letabundus* . . . . 60 *b*
Grounde take in vertue by Patriark*es* oldes.
. . .
This nowe yere doth þ*er* on Remembre.

17. *Incipiunt quindecim OO* . . . . 65 *b*
Blissid lorde my lorde O Ihū crist.
. . .
The charter asselid whan þou hing on þe Roode.

18. *Incipit oracio ad crucem* . . . . 70 *b*
In cruce sum pro te qui peccas desine pro me.

Desine do veniam sic culpam retraho penam.
Upon a cros nailed I was for the.
...
At hir request to vs be m*er*ciable.

19. *Incipit de sancta Maria* . . . . 71 *b*
O quene of heuen of hell eeke emp*er*es.
...
On Cristes passion and on hir Joyes fyve.

20. *Incipit de osculo sancto ad verbum caro factum est* . . . . 72 *b*
Ye deuout peple which kepe on obseruance.
...
Which for þi sake werid a croun of Thorn.
Printed in *Minor Poems*, p. 60, from another MS.

21. *Stella celi extirpauit* . . . . 73 *a*
Thou heuenly quene of grace oure lood sterre.
...
Saue all þi s*er*uantes from stroke of pestilence.

22. *Incipit de decim martiribus* . . . . 73 *b*
Blessed denys of Athenis chief sonne.
...
As þu art verray martir and virgyne.

23. *Incipit de sancto Leonardo* . . . . 75 *b*
Rest and refuge to folke disconsolate.
...
Where aungels were wont to syng Osanna.

24. *Incipit de tribus virginibus Katerina Margareta & Magdalena* 76 *a*
Katerina with glorious M*er*garete.
...
Ihū haue marcye when we on to þe call.

25. *Incipit de xi millibus virginibus* . . . . 76 *b*
Ye briton martirs famous in p*er*fitnes.
...
Vs to socoure lorde when we to þe call.

26. *Stans puer ad mensam* . . . . 77 *a*
My dere childe first þi self enable.
...
Put all defaute vpon John Lidgate.
Printed in *Rel. Ant.* i. 156, from this MS.

27. *Si deus est animus nobis ut carmina dicunt* . . . . . 78 *b*–92 *b*
Hic tibi precipue sit pura mente colendus.
For why þat god is inwardly þe witt.
...
Nat . . . . . . bot symplenes of witt.

Explicit liber Catonis.

57. Q. G. 9.

Collectio Errorum, etc.

Vellum, $7\frac{3}{4} \times 5\frac{1}{4}$, ff. 259, 38 lines to a page. English. Cent. xv. Binding: original, white skin over boards. Presented by Mr Man.

Collation: a^8–v^8 w^{12}–z^{12} aa^{18} bb^{12} cc^{16} (wanting 10, 11, 12 blank): 259 leaves.

Provenance: probably Durham. There are tags cut from the same MS. as in Q. B. 6. Not in *Catt. Vett.*

Contents:

1. Collectio errorum in anglia et parisius condempnatorum qui sic per capitula distinguuntur et primo de erroribus condempnatis in anglia . . . . f. 1

   Primum capitulum de erroribus in gramatica.

   Follows a table of the 21 chapters.

   Isti sunt errores condempnati a ffratre Roberto de Kyluarby archiepiscopo cantuar. de consensu omnium magistrorum tam regentium quam non regentium apud oxoniam die jouis proxima post festum sc̄i cuthberti in quadragesima • anno dn̄i millesimo • ducentesimo • septuagesimo sexto.

   De erroribus in gramatica primum capitulum.

   Ego currit, tu currit, etc.

   On f. 7*a* is a confirmation, and additions to the list, by John (Peckham) Abp of Canterbury, dated Ap. 30, 1286.

2. Table, in another hand, to the next item 8
3. Thomas Aquinas de malo 9

The heading, partly cut off, is:

R (? N) Thomas de malo ....

Ends on f. 166*a*.

ff. 166*b*, 167*b* have scribbles: on 168*b* is a list of books:

Isti sunt libri quos emit Thomas de Wyniston oxonie. Tota summa Thome de Aquino in quatuor uoluminibus videl. Prima pars summe per se • prima secunde per se • *secunda secunde* (erased) per se et tercia pars per se •1• ultima pars. Totum scriptum eiusdem Thome super sentencias in tribus uoluminibus, videl. primum scriptum super primum sent. et scriptum super secundum sent. in vno volumine.

Item scriptum super tercium sent. in vno volumine per se et scriptum super quartum sent. per se sed finis eiusdem scripti scil. a quadragesima distinctione exclusiue usque ad finem ligatur cum ultima parte summe.

Item liber qui intitulatur contra gentiles per se. et est eiusdem Thome de Aquino.

Item tabula super libros n*ot*a*bi*les. et liber qui intitulatur de ueritate in vno volumine.

Item questiones egidij de esse et essencia & de cognitione angelorum et de mensura angelorum. & questiones egidij super primum sentenciarum .s. usque ad vicesimam primam distinctionem • et questiones bartholomei super decreta et tabubula super originalia in vno volumine.

Item.... ra Thome de Aquino super quatuor libros sentent.: et questiones fratris Willelmi de Ware super quatuor libros sent. in vno volumine.

Item summa fratris minoris nomine de media villa hoc est de menevyl et questiones eiusdem de quolibetis. et questiones fratris egidij de quolibetis • et questiones fratris Willelmi de heyham disputate in scolis et determinate.

Item questiones fratris Tome de Aquino de spiritualibus creaturis.

Item • 7 • quolibeta eiusdem. Item de potencia. Item (erasure) ...s henrici de gandauo improbate. Item 21 questiones de anima • Thome. Item questiones fratris egidij super primum sent. s. 19 distinctiones. Item tractatus fratris Roberti (Kilwardby erased) herford.

Item questiones fratris R. de Kilwardby super sent.

Item postille super { psalterium / lucam / epistolas pauli } fratris nicholay de goram.

Item Ricardus de trinitate (Erasures.)

(Erasure) | questiones super librum
Liber de malo
hoc est iste liber
corruptorium per se
(erasure) magistri h. de gandauo in duobus uoluminibus.
cum probacione sua
volumina....

4. Tractatus de peccato mortali . . . . f. 169*a*
Quoniam sicut habetur deut° 25.
In another hand.
An Index at the end.

The original Table of Contents runs thus:

1. Errores in diuersis scientijs condempnati parisius et in anglia.
2. Questiones de malo cum titulis questionum preuiis.
3. Tractatus bonus de peccato mortali et veniali et ceteris peccati speciebus cum titulis questionum et tabula vocali in fine.

58. Q. G. 10.

Scala Chronica.

Vellum, 9¼ × 6½, ff. 87; part i., 2 columns of 32 lines each; part ii., 2 columns of 33 lines each. Cent. xiv.

Binding: modern.

Collation: a^8 (wants 1 and 4) b^8 c^8 d^8 e^8 f^8 g^8 h^8 i^8 || k^{12} l^6 (wants 6).

Contents:

1. The Scala Chronica of Thomas Gray (d. 1369?), in French prose, imperfect at the beginning. Partly edited by Stevenson for the Maitland Club. The principal MS. is at Corpus Christi (Cambridge), no. 132 . . . . f. 1 *a*

The present copy is imperfect at the beginning. The first words are drount a brut de loranguise et del seruage. The first rubric (f. 49) is comment les deux freres mamp'z et Maulin estriuerent pour la terre.

This copy goes down to the death of Henry III. in 1272. The Corpus MS. ends in 1362.

2. A chronicle in Latin beginning in the year 1042 and ending (imperfectly) with the death of Simon de Montfort . . 71 *a*

The last quire is misbound: ff. 83, 84 are turned round: the true order is f. 82, 84 *b*, 84 *a*, 83 *b*, 83 *a*, 85–87.

Elizabeth pigott (xvi) is on the margin of f. 40 *a*.

Thomas pigott est verus posser (*sic*) huius libri, f. 53 *a*.

This Chronicle is extracted from the important Annals of Waverley, a Cistercian house near Farnham. These Annals were edited by Dr Luard for the Rolls Series from the MS. in the Cottonian Collection.

The present text is shorter and begins at a later date, but the source is unmistakeable: cf. a MS. at Magd. Coll. Oxford, (no. cxcix.)[1].

The text begins on p. 180, ed. Luard, and ends with the words Henrici filij, p. 365, ed. Luard.

There is a xviith cent. transcript of this Chronicle in MS. Bodl. Tanner 383.

59. Q. G. 11.

Gulielmus Parisiensis, etc.

Vellum, $7\frac{1}{2} \times 5$, ff. 151, 42 lines to a page. Cent. xv.

Given by Mr Man.

Binding: 2 double leaves of a xiiith cent. Psalter, containing parts of Psalms lxxxviii–cxlii.

Collation: a^8–s^8 t^6 (+ 3* non distinguentes): 151 leaves.

Provenance: Durham. On f. 10 *a* is the inscription, de co*m*-*muni* libraria monachor*um* dunelm. Occurs in the Catalogue of

[1] Compare also a chronicle in Bodl., Laud. Misc. 564, Hardy, *Catalogue of Materials*, iii. 208.

1395, *Catalogi Veteres*, p. 72, Libraria claustralis, with the letter C and "ii fo., intelligitur."

Contents: there are two tables of contents, one of cent. xv on f. 1 *b*, one of cent. xvii on f. 1 *a*.

1. In principio librorum biblie et quot capita quibus libris continentur . . . . f. 2 *a*
2. Meditacio cuiusdam sapientis de custodia interioris hominis. Ad interioris hominis custodiam insinuandam . . . . 2 *b*
3. Notulae excerptae de diversis Doctoribus . . . . . 5 *a*
   One from Ricardus heremita de Aluernia Episc.
4. Willelmus Parisiensis de fide et legibus, in five books . . 10 *a*
5. Dialogus de deo et anima ex Trismegisto. Asclepius iste pro solo . . . . 135 *b*
6. An extract: anime non ex traduce procreantur . . . . 140 *a*
7. Confessio Joh. Wickliff de sacramento altaris. Corpus christi est idem . . . . 140 *b*
8. Extract: Omnes debemus laudare dominum . . . . . 144 *b*
9. De sacerdotum negligentia in divinis officiis celebrandis. Dolens refero 145
10. Excerpta e Patribus de oratione . . . . 146 *b*
11. 'Alueredus' (Ailred of Rievaulx) de anima . . . . . 147 *a*
12. Tractatus de mundo fugiendo. Diuina nobis monita . . 149 *a*
13. Extracts: de peccato originali . . . . 150 *a*
    On 151 *b* is the distich:

    No weyll wyll do & do no mys
    Fle fro evyll felyschyp were so euer it ys.

Nos. 1–3 and 6–13 are in one hand, no. 4 in a smaller hand, no. 5 possibly in the same, but in different ink.

60. Q. G. 12.

MEDICA.

Vellum and paper, $8\frac{1}{8} \times 5\frac{1}{4}$, ff. 316, 37 lines to a page. Cent. xv. Modern binding.

Collation: a^{8} (vellum) b^{20} (1, 20, 10, 11 vellum) c^{20} (1, 20, 10, 11 (vellum) d^{20} (1, 20, 10, 11 vellum) e^{20} (1, 20, 10, 11 vellum) f^{20} (1, 20, 10, 11 vellum) g^{20} (ut sup.) h^{20} (ut sup.) i^{20} (ut sup.) k^{20} (ut sup.) l^{8} (1, 8, 5, 6 vellum) m^{22} (1, 22, 11, 12 vellum) n^{20} (1, 20, 10, 11 vellum) o^{20} (ut sup.) p^{20} (ut sup.) q^{12} (1, 12, 6, 7 vellum) r^{20} (1, 20, 10, 11 vellum) s^{8} (wants 6, 7, not lost): 316 (1–8: 1–308).

Contents:

The verses on f. 282 *b* run thus:

Non didici gratis nec musa sagax Ipocratis
Egris in stratis seruiet absque datis.
Empta solet care multas medicina iuuare
Siqua datur gratis nil confert vtilitatis.
Res dare pro rebus pro verbis verba solemus
Pro vanis uerbis montanis vtimur herbis.
Pro caris rebus pigmentis et speciebus
Dum dolet infirmus medicus sit pignore firmus.
Instanter quere nummos uel pignus habere
Fedus in antiquum conseruiat pignus amicum
Nam si post queris querens inimicus haberis.

61. Q. G. 13.

Regula S. Benedicti, etc.

Vellum, 8 × 5¼, ff. 105, 31 lines to a page. Cent. xv, xiv.

Wooden binding: re-backed: clasp: formerly covered with skin.

Given by Mr Man.

From Durham. On f. 8 *a* is:

Venerabilis magister monachus et professus dominus Johannes ffysshburn cancellarius ecclesie cath. Dunelm. Obiit pridie Idus maij anno domini millesimo cccc° xxx° quarto. cuius anime propicietur deus. amen.

There is a rude sketch in black and red of a monk's head and "*John ffysshburn*" written beneath.

Below is:

Liber Johannis hamsterly (over an erasure) monachi Dunelm. disce pati.

On 9 *b* is:

Dominus Johannes (erasure) monachus eccl. cath. Dunellm.

On 10 *a* is:

Ister liber assignatur Almarolo nom*ine* ... per venerabilem patrem magistrum huttone priorem ecc. cath. dunelm.

Collation: i^8 a^{14} (14 cancelled) b^{12} c^8 || d^6 || e^{12} f^{12} g^6 || h^{12} || i^8 || k^{12} (wants 9, 10, 12).

Contents:

1. ff. 1–8 are fly-leaves made up of parts of Durham account-rolls (xv). The years to which they refer are not mentioned; the headings which remain are:

Decima garb. paroch. de Pyttyngton
Byllyngham
Aclyff.
Visitacio ecclesiarum
Decima garb. paroch. de Jarow
Wermouth
Hesilden.
Vendicio lane
garmann
corrij
feodi brasing
feodi coquine.
Recepcio fornic.
...ad firmam dimiss.
Empcio brasing
pisarum et fabe
vini
equorum
frumenti
Decima garb. paroch. de heyghynton
Estmeryngton
Aluerton
Estryngton
Loughall.

2. Table to the following work . . . . 9 *b*

3. Regula S. Benedicti . . . . 11 *a*
4. Appendix in another hand. De monachis et canonicis regularibus et monialibus . . . . 37 *b*
f. 41 was a double leaf: 41* is now loose.
5. A table to no. 7 in 30 divisions . . . . 41 *b*
6. Articuli super quibus in visitacione foret inquisicio facenda (*sic*). In a later hand . . . . 42 *a*
7. A tract headed C. R. D. A.
Christi subueniat michi mater ut hoc bene fiat . . . 48 *a*
From the table we gather that the book was known as:
Libellus 'Abbas uel prior' sic a suo principio nominatus. The opening words are 'Abbas uel prior': it is in 20 chapters with a prologue: in a hand of cent. xiv.
8. The table . . . . 69 *b*
9. A circular letter from the Abbots of S. Alban's, S. Mary's at York, S. Werburg at Chester, and others, to the Benedictines of England. Cent. xv.
Reyner. Apostolat. Bened. App. Script. 70 . . . . . 76 *a*
10. A similar letter from the Abbot of S. Alban's . . . 88 *a*
Printed l. c. App. Script. 75.
11. Rubrica de modo et forma procedendi in eleccione que obseruatur in practica secundum consuetudinem anglie. Licet circa diuersas . . . . 96 *a*
12. An explanation of the system of Arabic numerals . . . 103 *b*
13. Utrum liceat prelato absque consensu sui conuentus obseruanciarum dispensaciones siue mutaciones facere . . . 104 *a*

62. Q. G. 14.

PROCESSIONALE.

Vellum, 8 × 5½, ff. 46, 27 lines to a page. Cent. xv.

Modern binding.

A fragment of a Sarum Processional, noted: the leaves are bound in complete disorder.

The true order is as follows:

ff. 39–46 quire *e* = *Processionale*, ed. Henderson 51, Palm Sunday.

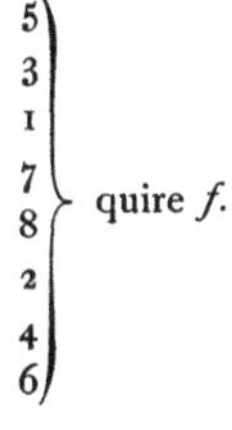

16–23 quire *e*.
24–31 quire *f*.
32–35 quire *g* (5 wanting).
One leaf lost (*Processionale*, pp. 117–119, Rogations).
36–38
9–15 quire *h* (wants 8: ends on p. 131 Henderson, Assumption).
The signatures *e*, *f* are repeated.

The collation runs thus: e^8 f^8 (misbound) e^8 f^8 g^8 (wants 5) h^8 (wants 8): 46 leaves.

The writing is fairly good: there is no decorative work.

63. Q. G. 15.

POGGII EPISTOLAE, ETC.

Paper, 7½ × 5½, ff. 76, 18 lines to a page. Cent. xv, late.

Given by Mr Man.

Binding: parchment over wooden boards: strap and pin fastening (gone). At least two quires of vellum gone at the beginning. Resembles the Bury books in respect of binding and general appearance.

Collation: a^{16} (wants 1) b^{16} c^{16} d^{20} e^{12} (wants 10, 11, 12): 76 leaves.

Contents:

Epistola barnardi ad Raymundum militem de cura et modo rei familiaris vtilius gubernande . . . . f. 1 *a*
Letter on the death of Galeotus . . . . 3 *b*
Dux Mediolani . . . . 4 *b*
Epistolae Pogij oratoris illustrissimi . . . . 5 *a*

1. Petro Dondito Ep. Castellano.
2. Johanni Aretino.
3. Franc. Barbaro.
4. Leonardo Aretino. At the top is the rubric:

   Ricardo Secretario Epi. Wynton.
5. Leonardo Aretino.
6. Joh. Pratensi.
7. Franc. Marescall. Ferrariens.
8. Cosmo de Medicis.
9. Nich. Lusco.
10. Guarino.
11. Valasco Portugalensi.
12. To the same.
13. Guarino.

14. Victurino.
15. Illustri principi D. Joh. Franc. Marchioni Mantue.
16. Carolo Aretino.
17. Leon. Aretino.
18. Leon. Estensi.
19. Guarinus Leonello Estensi.
20. Poggius Franc. Barbaro.

Illustriss. et literatiss. principi et domino D. humffredo duci gloucestrie. Si velimus tociens . . . . 26 *a*

To the same from Thomas de campo fregoso Januensis dux . . 27 *a*

At the end (26 *b*):

Amen quod Tpmbs brmkn = Tomas Armin.

Dilucidarium lemonocensis (sc. Joh. Lemovicensis) de sompno pharaonis . . . . 28 *a*

This is a tract dedicated to Theobald King of Navarre, and printed by Wagenseil, and also by Fabricius (*Cod. Pseud. V. T.* i. 441). It is of frequent occurrence. It consists of 20 letters, which are supposed to be written by Joseph, Pharaoh, the chief butler, the magicians, the courtiers, and Joseph's detractors.

Ends on 73 *b*. Scribbles follow on three blank leaves: the name Gregory Knagges is repeated. Some farm accounts follow, and a letter to Maister ffrancis Thornill to say "my brother Thomas Fairwether has chosen you to be on his Jury concerning the sute between him and contlas."

64. Q. G. 16.

Boethius de Trinitate, etc.

Vellum, $7\frac{5}{8} \times 5$, ff. 119, 37 lines to a page. Cent. xii.

Given by Mr Man.

Bound in a leaf of a folio book of Canon Law with text and comment. Cent. xiv. Two pairs of leather tags serve to fasten it.

Collation: a^8 b^8 (7, 8 blank, wanting) ‖ c^{10}–i^{10} ‖ k^8–n^8 (+ 7*) o^2.

Provenance: Northern. The book strongly resembles nos. 52, 53. The name of the monastery that owned it has been erased on f. 2 *b*.

Contents:

1. Boetii liber de Trinitate . . . . f. 3 *a*
   preceded by
   Table of contents (cent. xvii) . . . . 1 *b*
   Extracts about Boetius (cent. xii) . . . . . . 2 *a*
   Table of contents in red (cent. xii, xiii) . . . . . 2 *b*

2. Eiusdem Epistola ad S. Johannem Diaconum Eccl. Rom. an tres personae de diuinitate substantialiter praedicentur . 5 *b*
3. Eiusdem Epistola ad eundem quomodo substantiae in eo quod sint, bonae sint, cum non sint substantialia bona . . 6 *a*
4. Eiusdem Confessio fidei christianae . . . . . . 7 *a*
5. Eiusdem de Persona et Natura . . . . 9 *a*
f. 15 *b* is blank.
6. Anselmi Monologion . . . . 16 *a*
7. Anselmi Proslogion . . . . 39 *b*
8. Eiusdem de incarnatione uerbi . . . . 50 *a*
9. Eiusdem Prefacio in subditos tractatus . . . . . . 58 *a*
10. Tractatus de ueritate . . . . 58 *b*
11. De libertate arbitrii . . . . 64 *b*
12. De casu diaboli . . . . 70 *b*
f. 84 *a*, 85 *b* are blank: 84 *b*, 85 *a* are covered with notes in pencil of cent. xiv, xv.
13. Eiusdem. Libri ii contra gentiles, cur deus homo . . 86 *a*
14. De conceptu virginali et originali peccato . . 109 *a*
Two blank leaves at end, with scribbles.

65. Q. G. 17.

EXPOSITIO MISSAE, ETC.

Vellum, $7\frac{1}{2} \times 5\frac{1}{2}$, ff. 71 (69 numbered), 30 lines to the page for the most part. Cent. xii, xiii.

Given by Mr Man.

Binding: a leaf of a folio Psalter in double columns, cent. xiii, the same book in which nos. 20 and 25 are bound. The fly-leaves are from the smaller Psalter, which has been used to bind Q. G. 4 and 5. At the beginning is the middle sheet of a quire containing parts of Pss. xli. (xlii.) *Judica me*—xliv. (xlv.) *Deus auribus.* At the end is a sheet containing parts of Pss. xxxiii. *Exultate iusti,* xxxvi. *Noli emulari.*

The provenance of this and the other books in which fragments of this Psalter recur is probably Durham.

This is probably the volume described on p. 25 of *Catt. Vett.* "D. Exp. missae cum sermonibus et quodam tract. de officiis ecclesiasticis ii. fo., *ant' quasi.*"

Collation: a^{10} b^{8}–f^{8} g^{6} (wants 1) h^{8} i^{8}.

Contents:

1. Expositio misse. In uirtute sancte crucis . . . . . f. 1
26 lines to a page.

2. Extracts: on leprosy . . . . 8 *b*
on the Holy Ghost given to the Apostles . . 9 *a*
Notes in a very small hand, 9 *b*.
3. Sermons:
1. Sermo Gibuini de filio prodigo. Fili mi, memorare . 10 *a*
2. Et nunc reges intelligite . . . . 10* *a*
3. Sicut portauimus . . . . 10* *b*
4. Dom. Quinquagesime. Egredere de terra . . . 10* *b*
Adorna thalamum . . . . 11 *b*
4. Extracts . . . . 12 *a*
5. Sermo in Annunciatione dominica. Conuerti me ad portam . 17 *a*
6. Sermo in festo Apostolorum Petri et Pauli. Transiens autem primam . . . . 19 *a*
7. Sermo in Purificacione B. M. Postquam impleti. Uolumus dilecti gratia . . . . 21 *a*
8. Sermo Synodalis. Erudimini qui iudicatis terram . . 23 *a*
9. Sermon, Surge qui dormis . . . . 25 *a*
10. Sermo in Quadragesima. Dixi confitebor . . . . . 26 *b*
11. „ in die Epiphanie. Qui sedes super cherubin . . 28 *b*
12. Sermon for Pentecost. Spiritus domini impleuit . . . 29 *b*
13. Sermo in Assumptione B. M. Tota pulcra...Presens gloriose virginis . . . . 31 *a*
14. Extract. Legitur quod septem populos . . . . . 32 *b*
15. Sermon, Omnis caro corruperat . . . . 33 *a*
16. „ Vie syon lugent . . . . 34 *a*
17. „ In hunc modum loquitur patres . . . . . 35 *a*
18. De institutione misse et de intellectu eorum que in ea continentur et ordine oracionum. Introitus sacerdotis... . 36 *a*
19. Rubric gone. Ut intinguatur pes tuus . . . . . . 37 *a*
20. „ Oritur sol et occidit . . . . . . 37 *b*
21. Sermo in dedicatione ecclesie. Domum tuam decet . . 38 *b*
22. Rubric gone. Intrauit ihesus in quoddam castellum . . 39 *b*
23. Sermon on the parable of the Vineyard (Matt. xx.) . . 41 *a*
24. „ Ite baptizate . . . . 42 *b*
25. „ Cum inuitatus fueris ad nuptias . . . . . 43 *a*
26. Dom. i. post octavam Pentecostes. Temptatus est ihesus . 44 *a*
27. „ iii. „ „ „ Que mulier habens dragmas . . . . 45 *a*
28. Three extracts . . . . 45 *b*
29. Sermo in Quadragesima. Utinam appenderentur . . . 46 *a*
30. Dominica .xiij. Et approprians samaritanus. Hec sunt uerba . . . . 47 *b*
31. Quid sit fides . . . . 48 *c*
32. Exposition of some Levitical ceremonies . . . . . 49 *a*
In two columns of 32 lines.
33. Sermo in Dom. palmarum. Dauid futura spiritu preuidens . 52 *a*
34. Sermo magistri Petri in.... Surge aquilo, 35 lines to a page 54 *a*
35. Miscellaneous extracts . . . . 55 *a*

36. Sermon. Sumetur de sanguine agni . . . . . . 57 *b*
37. Extracts . . . . 58 *b*
38. Incipit de xij apostolis ubi nati fuerint et in quibus terris predicauerint et quomodo martirio coronati sint . . . 59 *a*
39. Questiones de diuersitate in officiis ecclesiasticis . . . 59 *b*
Querendum est quis primum clericus factus est in memoriam dominice passionis.
The hand changes on 60 *a* to double columns of 45 lines.
Ends imperfectly on 69 *b*: Quare in prima non recitatur lectio post psalmos ut in aliis horis. Quia sicut psalmi.

66. Q. G. 18.

PETRI CANTORIS TROPI, ETC.

Vellum, $6\frac{7}{8} \times 5$, ff. 77 + 5, double columns of 39 lines. Cent. xiii, xiv.

Given by Mr Man.

Binding: one cover remains of cent. xvii? stamped with a gold pheasant in the centre, which according to Mr Jenkinson is a Cambridge binder's mark.

Collation: a^{12} b^{12} c^{14} d^{8} (wants 3) e^{8} (wants 4, 5) f^{10} (wants 4) g^{10} h^{8} (wants 8): 77 leaves.

Provenance: seemingly Durham, to judge by the hand in which the title of the first tract is written.

Contents:

1. Tropi magistri petri cantoris parisius:
Videmus nunc per speculum et in enigmate . . . f. 1 *a*
2. Svbtilis exposicio simboli traditi a beato anastio (sc. Athanasio). Sicut ait apostolus fides est . . . . . . 39 *a*
3. Exposicio parui simboli s. laicorum:
Quoniam ut ait Augustinus . . . . . . 43 *a*
In another hand: headed sancti spiritus assit nobis gratia.
Exposicio parui simboli explicit. Incipit representacio temporum que finierunt ab inicio mundi usque ad finem pȝ · ꝑ · un · li · q> · fa · qᵗ. On two leaves (e 4, 5) which are gone.
4. Sentencia dominice orationis exposita breuiter nec non vtiliter. vbi tanguntur · vii · peticiones prout comparantur · vii · donis spiritus sancti.
Licet sciat deus . . . . 49 *a*
5. Sententia beati Roberti lincolniensis episcopi de fide et articulis fidei incipit . . . . 50 *b*

The fly-leaves are from a MS. of similar form and date. They consist of five leaves. The first four are the two middle sheets of a quire, apparently a treatise on preaching.

f. 1 *a* ends with a rubric: de confirmacione modorum. Consequenter redeamus predictos modos confirmantes.

2 *a* quomodo hiis modis hñdemus.

2 *c* de supplemento dictorum modorum, on the interpretation of names. Agnaes quasi agna es ut per agnam innuatur eius innocencia similiter eadburg quasi ediburg quasi beata ciuitas similiter in Gallico tresor quasi tre sord cui consonat quod temporalia a sanctis dicuntur stercora.

Ends on 3 *b*: sed sufficit procede ut procedit ecclesiasticus.

3 *b* Augustinus de latrone pendente in cruce.

4 *b* Sermo de S. Maria V. Sicud dicit hillarius.

f. 5 begins: sic plane verus amor morbus est,

ends 5 *b*: in ha musica et beatificatur tota celestis curia ad quam uos perdicat deus etc. Amen. Col. 2 blank.

67. Q. G. 19.

Wallensis Communeloquium, etc.

Vellum, $7\frac{1}{8} \times 5\frac{1}{2}$, ff. 228, 33 lines to a page. Cent. xiv.

Given by Mr Man.

Binding: two sheets of a Psalter of cent. xiii. Large hand, single lines, containing parts of Pss. Confitemini Super flumina || Laetatus sum and Ad te levavi || In conuertendo || Laudate nomen.

Collation: a^{12} b^{12} c^{8} d^{12}–t^{12} u^{4}.

Provenance: no doubt Durham. The hand of the title is unmistakable.

Contents:

On f. 1 *a* is:

> G. Communeloquium Wallensis G. Et oculus moralis cum tabula eiusdem in fine.

In *Catt. Vett.* p. 77, we find G. Communeloquium Wallensis: et Tractatus de oculo morali: cum tabula super Comm. Wall. in fine: ii fo. "rerum accepcione."

1. Hic incipit tractatus qui dicitur summa collectionum . . f. 1 *a*

Ends on f. 168 *b*:

> Expl. tractat. qui dicitur commune loquium (in another hand) compositus a fratre Joh. Walensi de ord. fratr. minorum qui quidem Johannes socius erat Johannis Kidinnas.

2. Two extracts:
   (*a*) Repletus spiritus sancti gratia.
   (*b*) Hugo de claustro anime. Hec sunt ille fenestré . . 168 *b*
   f. 169 *b* is blank.
3. Oculus moralis per Lincoln. . . . . 170 *a*
4. Table in two columns . . . . 225 *b*
   f. 228 *b*:
   In isto volumine continentur summa Wanlensis et summa de oculo morali cum tabula (erasure).
   precium xl s.
   Fly-leaves: parts of five at beginning and three at end: double columns: small hand, cent. xiv: on baptism (?).

68. Q. G. 20.

AEGIDII SUMMA, ETC.

Vellum, 7 × 5, ff. 148, varying numbers of lines. Cent. xiii, xiv.
Given by Mr Man.
Binding: modern.
Provenance: Durham (?).
Collation: ii^{12} iii^{12} $iiij^{10}$ v^{12} || i^{12} ii^{12} iii^{16} $iiij^{12}$ v^{6} || a^{4} b^{12}–d^{12} e^{4}.

Contents:

1. Notule Decretalium: an analysis of the Decretals in 5 books . f. 1 *a*
   The first quire (of 12 leaves?) gone: in two columns of 42 lines.
2. Miscellaneous notes . . . . 46 *b*
3. Aegidii Foscarii summa juris canonici: in another hand, 45 lines to a page . . . . 47 *a*
   Ends on 101 *b*.

4. Notes in another hand: cases of canon law . . . . . 102 *a*
De modo intronizandi episcopum . . . . 104 *b*
Miscellaneous notes, much rubbed . . . . 105 *a*
105 *b* blank.

5. Libellus fugitiuus compositus a mag. nepote de monte albano: hand of no. 3.
At top: Liber magistri Henrici de Lutebÿr (?).
Ends on f. 145 *b*.

6. Extracts:
A statute (?): Attendens ego Benaguido . . . . . . 146 *a*
f. 147 blank.
f. 148 *a* Willelmus permissione diuina Norwycensis episcopus dilectis filiis Abbate et conuentui de Geng'l (Genling'): about the Churches of All Saints and S. Peter and the Chapel of S. Paul at Gesynh*a*m (Gesinh*a*m).
Between ff. 80, 81 is stitched a deed:

In dei nomine amen. Nos Ainer*us* permiss. diu. Linc. Eps. domine Sybille Maurewad Gilberto de Oleby et Roberto de Scepeye ex officio ad promocionem mag. Johannis de Melton (?) rectoris eccl. de Hauerhill executoris quondam mag. Joh. de Melton rectoris eccl. de *k*etelbÿ defuncti orrimus per presentes quod licet idem defunctus viginti libras annui redditus ad erogandum in pios usus per manus magr. Joh. executoris predicti in suo testamento rite condito et autoritate (?) cedinar', approbato legasset. dicti tamen Sibilla Gilbertus et Robertus uoluntatem memorati defuncti procedere usu sinentes immo dictum redditum ut prouenit penes se propriam detinentes vel alias solucionem eiusdem fieri executori predicto non permittentes ipsius testamenti execucionem impediunt manifeste. maiores (-is) excommunicacionis sentenciam in omnes tales a canone promulgatam dampnabiliter incurrendo super quo contra ipsos et eorum quemlibet ad anime coap • tionem intendimus ex officio procedere ad promocionem executoris predicti et statuere quod est iustum, eisque ac omnibus quorum interest exhibere iusticie complementum.

69. Q. G. 21.

SUMMA RAYMUNDI, ETC.

Vellum, 7 × 5, ff. 108, double columns of 48 lines. Cent. xiii, xiv.
Given by Mr Man.

Binding: original: brown leather over boards: strap and pin fastening.

Provenance: Durham.

Collation: a^{12}–i^{12}.

Contents:

1. On fly-leaves, notes and memorial verses, extracts from Aug. and Bernard.
2. Summa Raymundi de communi librario monachorum Dunelm. See *Catt. Vett.* p. 36, T. summa Raymundi ii fo., "Sacramenti." Ends on 105 *a*.
3. In another (later and larger) hand a tract on Marriage Law.
4. Quoniam frequenter in foro penitentiali dubitaciones circa matrimonium . . . . 105 *b*
   The end is gone: at least one quire is lost.

70. Q. G. 22.

ROBERTUS LINCOLNIENSIS IN BOETHIUM, ETC.

Vellum, $6\frac{3}{4} \times 5\frac{3}{8}$, ff. 122, 52 lines to a page, in a neat small running hand of cent. xv.

Given by Mr Man.

Binding: white vellum with a small stamp.

Provenance: probably Durham: not in *Catt. Vett.*

Collation: a^{12}–h^{12} i^{14}.

Contents:

1. Roberti Grosthead Commentum in Boetium de Consolatione Philosophiae . . . . f. 1 *a*
   There is a good initial and partial border of characteristic English work.
   Expl. comentum Mag. Rob. Grosthede lincolniensis episcopi super Boecio de philosophica consolacione. Deo gracias quod Robertus Emylton . . . . 89 *a*
2. Recapitulacio metrorum consolacionis philosophice Anicij mallij Seuerini boecij exconsulis ordinarij . . . . 89 *a*
3. Ambrosius de bono mortis . . . . 90 *b*
   Expl. libellus b. Ambrosij qui intitulatur de bono mortis. Deo gracias quod R. Emylton . . . . 100 *a*
4. Libellus hugonis de S. Victore de virtutibus et vicijs . . 100 *b*
   Expl. ...Deo gracias quod R. Emylton . . . . . . 107 *a*
5. Libellus Magistri hugonis de S. Victore de consciencia . . 107 *a*
   ...Deo gracias quod R. Emylton . . . . . 109 *a*
6. Lucij annei senece ad callionem de remedijs fortuitorium . 109 *a*
   ...Deo gracias quod R. Emylton . . . . . 111 *a*

A few marginal notes in a slightly later hand.

7. P. ovidii Nasonis de Vetula liber tercius . . . . . 111 *b*

Iste sunt cause propter quas ammodo nolo
Viuere sicut eram solitus nec subdere collum.

With some marginal notes in Emylton's hand.

Ends:

Pro nobis te non pigeat suadere quod ad te
Nos trahat is per te qui per te uenerit ad nos
Maxima quem per te dileccio traxerit ad nos
A nobis ipsi sit gloria laudis ab ipso
Gracia sit nobis et mete nescia vita.

Ouidij Nasonis pelignensis de vetula liber tercius explicit. duobus primis hic omissis propter multa que interseruntur scurrilia. Deo gracias quod R. Emylton . . . . . 119 *b*

8. Incipit tractatus et causa quare singula volumina sua composuit iste ouidius.

In librorum inicijs septem solent inquiri que ad causas • 4 • reducuntur—ideo in laudem illius virginis t*ermin*at librum suum . . . . 121 *b*

9. Sequitur eciam prefacio leonis prothonotarij que preponitur isti libello vt cercius appareat quod ouidius erat eius auctor.

Ovidius naso peligni ruris alumpnus
Certus ab exilio se iam non posse reuerti
Et querens quecumque sibi solacia librum
122 *a* Edidit hunc, in eo describens quis modus ipsi
Viuendi fuerat. tunc quum vacabat amori
Quare mutauit et quomodo postea vixit
Quidve intendebat simul ac ab amore vacauit
Imposuitque suo titulum nomenque libello
De vetula pro qua fuerat mutacio facta
Inque suo secum iussit condire sepulcro
Vt sua si saltem contingeret ossa referri
Cor redeunte libro rediuiuum nomen haberet
Sed quia nullus eis curauit de referendis
Nec fuit ante*m*ptim lectus nec habetur in vsu
Quaeritur unde mihi quod opus processerit istud
Versibus exametris solum nec subduplicatum
More meo pentememerim cum nullus herois (-um)
Hic describatur sed qui perlegerit ipsum
Sedulus inueniet seruiti semper amoris
A modo me debere iugo subducere. sic quod
Respondere sibi poterit cur euacuata
Causa debuerit cantus et euacuari
Versus amatorum proprius venerique dicatus.

Explicit prefacio leonis prothonotarij sacri palatij bizantei sub vacacio principe in librum Ouidij Nasonis pelignensis de vetula. Deo gracias quod R Emylton.

f. 122 *b*. A page of writing in a different hand. The beginning of a tract:

...estra nouit. Jntēº de scolarium disciplina compendiosum postulare tractatum.

A MS. by this scribe was sold in 1895 at the Phillipps sale at Sotheby's (lot 92). Compare no. 56 of the Sidney Sussex MSS.

71. Q. G. 24.

Ricardi de S. Victore Sermones, etc.

Vellum, $6\frac{7}{8} \times 5$, ff. 44, 21 and 25 lines to a page. Cent. xiii (early).

Given by Mr Man.

Binding: parchment over mill-boards.

Provenance: Durham. On 1 *a*: B. De communi libraria monachorum dunelm. super euangelium *Ductus est*. Thus entered in the Catalogue of 1395 (*Catt. Vett.* p. 75):

Sermo Ricardi de S. Victore super Euangelium *Ductus est Iesus in desertum a Spiritu* et omeliae Joh. Crisostomi super Euangelium *Egressus Iesus*. ii fo. appareret gracia.

Collation: a⁸–d⁸ e⁴.

Contents:

1. A Sermon on the Temptation.
   Ductus est ihesus in desertum a spiritu. De serie lectionis euuangelice sufficit hucusque. In sermone presenti non oportet progredi ultra . . . . f. 1 *a*
   ...Ibi ab ipso et in ipso et de ipso non homine sed deo id est non secundum ipsius humanitatem sed secundum ipsius diuinitatem saciatur plenarie apparente glorie illius plenitudine qui est gloriosus et benedictus in secula seculorum amen . . 34 *b*
   ff. 35, 36 blank.
2. Omelia beati Johannis Crisostomi de muliere Chananaea . . 37 *a*
   In another hand, 25 lines to a page. Ends on 44 *a*.

72. Q. G. 25.

Misc. Medica.

Vellum and paper, $6 \times 4\frac{1}{2}$, ff. 205, 27 lines to a page. Cent. xv (late).

Binding: limp vellum.

Collation: a[10] (v) b[38] (wants 3, 5, 10, 19, 20, 29, 34 v) c[36] (1, 8, 13, 18, 19, 24, 29, 36 v) d[32] (3, 5, 16, 17, 25, 30 v: wants 18) ff[34] (2, 4, 17, 18, 31, 33 v) g[8] (v: wants 8) h[24] (vellum guards outside and in middle) j[28] (1, 14, 15, 28 v).

Contents:

1. Receipts in English, almost illegible . . . . . . f. 1 *a*
   Receipts in Latin . . . . 1 *b*
2. Incipiunt notabilia distinctiones textus distinctiones librorum de anima extracte:
   (h)onor honorabilium noticiam opinantes . . . . . 14 *a*
   On the *L.* margin is a scroll: nauseat anima mea distia[nes] (=distinctiones).
   At the bottom, a grotesque human figure, and two dogs fighting.
   Primus liber de Anima:
   honor honorabilium actor Tractaturus philosophus de anima 15 *a*
   Secundus liber:
   Et quidem a prioribus tradita sunt Actor. Tractando de anima sed opiniones . . . . 19 *b*
   Explicit . . . . 33 *b*
   Quoniam a duabus drūcijs. Actor . . . . . . 33 *b*
   et sic terminatur liber 3[tius] de anima ad laudem creatoris animarum qui est deus benedictus per omnia secula seculorum. Amen.
   Explicit 3[tius] liber de Anima quod Sutton . . . . 41 *b*
3. Memorial verses, ? logical:
   hostem nouit euuolo • 9 • iuuat • agmina christi
   ffur • dampnum • repere • bene getilem • nouitatis . 42 *a*
4. Receipts in Latin, for stains on clothes etc. . . . . . 42 *b*
   and scribbles.
5. *Utrum logica sit scientia.* Quod non sit probatur Quia modus sciendi non est scientia . . . . 49 *a*
6. Hic incipiunt distincciones et notabilia extracta a questionibus super primum librum phisicorum Aristotelis.
   Primo notabile quod cuiuslibet casus existen*tis* rei . . . . 55 *a*
   On margin of 58 *a* a scroll: hic incipit primus liber phisicorum.
   Expl. quoddam compendium vtilissime extractum de 8. libris phisicorum q. t. s. . . . . 74 *a*
7. Receipts in Latin.
   Scribbles.
   A hymn: Stella celi / Mater meli / Vectrix veli } superne deitatis

   Pelle pestem / Pande vestem / Nunc celestem } donatrix sanitatis

Ora natum
Ne peccatum } carnis egritudine
Perpetratum

Quod nos fedat
Sanos ledat } dire mortis vlcere
Viuos cedat

8. Hic incipiunt notabilia extracta ex tercio de anima secundum Alexandrum . . . . 86 *a*
Notandum est sicut omne vi*detu*r.
Ends without explicit on 98 *b*.
9. Receipts in Latin . . . . 99 *a*
10. Without title. Primo est sciendum secundum M. henricum de mandavilla quod eodum modo operatur cecus in ligno et cirurgicus in corpore cuius anothomiam ignorat . . . . 115 *b*
Explicit Albertus super quedam dicta magistri henrici de mandevilla de anothomia corporis cum quibusdam superadditis . . . . 139 *b*
11. Receipts: the last (added) on 150 *a* ends with the words: pro moniali apud sherefhoton.
12. Arnaldus de noua uilla de gradibus . . . . . . 150 *b*
13. Receipts . . . . 152 *a*
14. A separate book of Receipts for the different parts of the body. Conferunt cerebro... Ends on 164 . . . . 155 *a*
15. Contenta magistri Walteri Agulini de urinis . . . . . 169 *a*
16. Receipts . . . . 175 *a*
Continued to end of volume.

73. Q. G. 26.

DICTIONARIUM THEOLOGICUM.

Vellum, $5\frac{3}{4} \times 4$, ff. 271 + 8, double columns of 29 lines each. Cent. xiv, xv.

Given by Mr Man.

Binding: the original wooden boards, no back.

Collation: i^4 (blank): a^8–m^8 n^8 (+ a slip) o^8–u^8 (wants 7) v^8–z^8 aa^8–kk^8: ii^4 (fly-leaves).

Contents:

A Theological Encyclopaedia:

Absolucio dicitur Z. scilicet absolucio autoritativa:
Zelus. ...ibi inconstancia et omne opus prauum.

The colophon (two lines) is erased.

ff. 264 *b*–268 *a* are blank: on 268 *b*, in col. 2, begins an extract:

Gladium appellat dolorem effectum dominice passionis. In marg.: haec bernardus.

Miscellaneous extracts follow to end of 271 *b*.

The fly-leaves at end are unfinished sheets of an English gloss on Psalm xvii. (xviii.), xvth cent.

Also: Iste liber pertinet ad me Wyllm̄ collywood (xv, xvi).

At beginning: Thomas Man 1651.

74. Q. G. 27.

WILLELMUS DE CONCHES SUPER BOETHIUM.

Vellum, $5\frac{3}{4} \times 3\frac{3}{4}$, ff. 129, 20 lines to a page. Cent. xv.

Binding: leather, xviith–xviiith cent.

Provenance. The following names occur: G. Blyth: sum liber Georgij Barcroft A malo fuge et fac bonum: Johannes Benn de Monden Magna in com. Hartfordiae et Sidnoei Collegij in Academia Cantabrigiensi alumnus Martij 16. 1620: Liber Collegij Jesu 1669. E. B.

Collation: a^8–g^8 (h i gone) k^6 l^8–o^8 p^8 (+ 8* sed duo) q^8 r^8 (s gone) t^{10}.

Contents:

Commentum Willelmi de conches super boecium de consolacione philosophie.

Boecius iste nobilissimus romanus ciuis.

On f. 129 *a*:

Remember Mistris Elis to Mr Rowsley for forti l. of hemp ter and he is payd for the sam forti pownds and he must send vpp twenti pownds mor and she will pay hym att mechealmas next following by the Graice of God.

In cover:

George Barcroft will borrow of any that dare lende
But to paye againe, he doth never intend
erased Wherefore the lender is verie vnwise
And the borrower a knave by good advice.

Below, *alia manu:*

Then the borrower's a knave and y^e^ lender a fool,
And for to learn witt hee had need go to schoole.

75. Q. G. 28.

OCULUS SPIRITUALIS, ETC.

Vellum, $5\frac{3}{4} \times 4\frac{1}{4}$, ff. 219, 29 lines to a page. Cent. xiii, xiv.

Given by Mr Man.

Binding: old stamped leather (fleurs-de-lys and two rosettes) on boards: clasp gone.

Provenance: Kirkstall. On f. 1 *a* is

Liber monachorum beate marie de kyrkestall.

On the verso of the last leaf: Liber sancte Marie de Kyrkestall' ex dono fratris Johannis de Driffeld' monachi • In die ascensionis domini • Anno domini • millesimo • ccc^{s} • xl^{o} • iiij • Ad memoriam inter fratres perpetuandam et animam precibus deo comendandam.

Collation: a^{12}–d^{12} e^{14} || f^{14} g^{14} h^{16} i^{16} k^{20} l^{20} m^{14} n^{12} (+ 2* mense) o^{10}–q^{10}.

Contents:

Tractatus de oculo spirituali	f. 1
Table	61 *b*
Table to the following work	63 *a*
Medulla philosophorum. *Inc.* Cum omne desiderii	69 *b*
Table to the following work	198 *b*
Tract without title (De uirtutibus)	199 *b*
Cap. 1 De uirtute q*uere*ntium ad quatuor suas causas.	
Cap. ult. De eternitate felicitatis.	

Fly-leaves: *a.* adhering to first cover: a leaf of a chronicle in small hand (xiii, xiv). The year 968 and the names Lotharius Nicholaus Adrianus occur. It is largely obscured by the book plate.

b. A leaf and a half of Interpretationes nominum (xiii).

c. At end, parts of two leaves in two columns (xii, xiii) of a Psalter or service-book, giving the beginnings of the verses of the Psalms *Vsquequo domine* to *Expectans expectaui* in a large rough hand.

76. Q. G. 29.

S. HIERONYMUS AD DEMETRIADEM, ETC.

Vellum, $4\frac{3}{4} \times 3\frac{5}{8}$, ff. 230, 20 lines to a page. Cent. xii.

Binding: leather of cent. xvii (?) over original boards, formerly fastened with strap and pin.

Given by Mr Man.

Collation: a^8 b^8 c^8 (+ 8*) d^8 e^8 (+ 2 slips) f^8–k^8 l^{10} m^8 n^8 o^{10} p^8–r^8 s^8 (+ 1) t^8 (wants 1) u^6 v^4 (+ 2*) x^4 (wants 2, 4) y^{16} (wants 9–12) z^8 aa^8–dd^8.

Provenance. The book is from Durham. On f. 1 *a* is written *Eple Jeronimi ad demetriedem v'ginem .D.*, in a hand which is found in others of the Durham MSS. in this collection.

In the *Catt. Vett.* p. 94, we have:

D. Ep. Jeronimi ad Demetriedem Virginem. Dicta Anselmi. Sermo Augustini de Poenitentia. Meditationes Ancelmi. Prosologion eiusdem. Aug. de Praesentia Dei. Seneca de Institutione Morum. Collatio Serapionis de Vestimentis Sacerdotalibus. Tractatus de arte metrica. Item Compotus Practica Geometriae et Lamentationes Jeremiae. ii. fo. *considerare.*

Contents:

Epistola Hieronymi ad Demetriadem Virginem . . . . . f. 1

Dicta Anselmi Archiepiscopi . . . . 21 *b*

Sermo S. Augustini de penitentia . . . . 23 *b*

Inc. Penitentes. penitentes. penitentes. si estis penitentes.

Collaterales iiii^or^ virtutum 25

Prudentia habet in dextro latere astutiam et uersutiam in sinistro autem habitudinem mentis. Justicia nanque habet in dextro latere pleonesiam hoc est plus iusto. In sinistro uero meonesyam hoc est minus iusto. Fortitudo itaque (*corr. for* nanque) habet in dextro latere audaciam. In sinistro ignauiam. Temperantia igitur habet in dextro latere castitatem et continentiam: in sinistro uero lxxxrkbm (= luxuriam) et lkbkdknfm (= libidinem).

De xii lapidibus 25

Inc. Ciues celestis patrie | regi regum concinite | qui est supremus artifex | ciuitatis uraniee.

Orationes siue meditationes Anselmi archiepiscopi 26

In another hand. They are entitled: ad Dominum, ad S. Mariam, ad S. Petrum, ad S. Paulum, ad S. Iohannem, ad S. Stephanum, ad S. Mariam Magd.: meditatio peccatoris ad excitandum timorem: deploratio uirginitatis male amisse: pro amicis priuatis: de se ipso.

Expl. monologion Anselmi arch.: Inc. prologus in proslogion eiusdem . . . . 73 *b*

Capitula 75

Proslogion Anselmi . . . . 75 *b*

Liber B. Augustini de presentia summi et ueri ac omnipotentis dei . 91

Seneca de institutione morum.

Inc. Omne peccatum actio est . . . . 104 *b*

Collatio Serapionis . . . . 113 *b*

Inc. Octo sunt principalia uitia.

f. 117 *b* is blank.

De vestimentis sacerdotalibus.

Amictus est primum uestimentum 118

An exposition of the Canon of the Mass.

FINIS EST AMHN.

150 *b* is blank.

A tract on Prosody: the first leaf of the prologue is gone. *Inc.* iuxta illud iuuenalis. Magna equidem sacris que dat precepta libellis Uictrix fortune sapientia: dicimus autem: Hos quoque felices. Ecce quos laudat poeta 151

The text begins on f. 151 *b* with the rubric *hic incipiunt dictiones metrificandi.* Omne metrum certis pedum mensuris terminatur.

Elegiac verses on death (30 lines) . . . . 171 *b*

Non pretexta toge, non aula case, nec amici
Est memor eximii cum quis ad alta uolet
Sic homo cum moritur, cum gleba quiescit in urna
Cum cinis in cinerem transit amicus abest.

A dialogue on Prosody 172

Omnibus o iuuenes uobis scripsi documenta
Vos facient memores fuerint si corde retenta.

Unus interrogat Omnibus: quis pes est? *Alter respondet* Dactilus.

Verses.

Uespere lux oritur et sole cadente diescit
Ortus in occasum tendit, phebus tenebrascit
Dum uiuens moritur Willelmus, celica celum
Pars tenet, illud humi debita soluit humo.

Ends on 176 *b*:

Vita breuis, labor, et finis, mors certa futura,
Judicium domini, nos suadent spernere mundum.

Verses in another hand (a quire lost) 177

Interius quid agat is • uocat ille foris
Caros illustrat sensu, succendit amore
Et mox lingua patet omnibus omnis eis
In terras omnes subito sonus exit eorum
Que sermone sonant actibus illa probant.
(On the Apostles, 35 lines remain.)

Hymn to the Virgin . . . . 177 *b*

Concinat omnis aue tibi psallant singula salue
Stella maria maris nescia nempe paris.

Ends:

Cui sit uita salus regnum lux gloria uirtus
Pax honor imperium laus decus et iubilum. Amen . . 178 *b*

Two lines follow:

> Tres obolos siclus, siclos tres dragma, sed octo
> Vncia dat dragmas duodena dat uncia libram.

Prologue to a treatise on astronomy, in another hand . . 179
Ut testatur ergaphalau. Absoluta non potest haberi alicuius rei noticia.
Text headed Sancti Spiritus assit nobis gratia . . . . 181 *b*
Spera est rotundum et globosum corpus.
Ends with directions for making an astrolabe.
f. 191 *b* is blank.
Gloss on the Lamentations, in another hand, has suffered from damp: ends on f. 226, four blank leaves (the last doubled) at end 192

77. Q. G. 30.

DIURNALE EBORACENSE.

Paper, 4 × 3, ff. 238, 22 lines to a page. Cent. xv (late).

Binding: white skin over boards, with bronze clasp, in white skin cover with flap running round it.

Given by Mr Man.

Imperfect at the beginning.

Inc. nostra operacio sed a te semper incipiat et per te
cepta finiatur. Per.
Nunc sancte nobis spiritus...
Legem pone....

Collation: a? b^6 (+ 1*) c^6 (wants 6) d^{12} e^{18} (wants 5, 6) f^{18} g^{12} (wants 9) h^{10} i^{10} (+ 10*) k^{12}–m^{12} n^{10} o^{12} p^{10} q^{12} r^{10} s^8 t^{10} u^{10} v^8 x^{10} y^{10} z^8 (4–8 blank).

The *Proprium de tempore* ends on f. 114.

In the *Proprium sanctorum* the following English saints are commemorated:

SS. Thomas, Cuthbert, Wilfrid, John of Beverley, Swythun, Oswald, John of Bridlington, Edward, Edmund.

The Feast of the Relics is placed immediately after S. Luke's day.

The *Commune Sanctorum* begins on f. 194 *b*.

There is a collect for S. William on f. 215 *b*.

On ff. 216 *b* sqq. are the half-verses of the Psalms for Vespers *Dixit dominus* etc. (cix.–cl.).

On ff. 223 *b* sqq. is the Office of the Dead.

The fly-leaves are from a xivth century MS. partly of historical import (the building of the church of Hypapante at Constantinople and the plague in the time of Mauricius are mentioned), partly homiletical.

The name of Thomas Thormu*n*by (xv) occurs on the last leaf.

LIST OF DONORS OF MANUSCRIPTS.

Mr Man, Fellow (date of gift, Jan. 21, 1685), 1, 6, 8, 13–16, 20, 22–25, 28–31, 34, 35, 38, 40, 41, 44, 45, 48, 50–57, 59, 61, 63–71, 73, 75–77

Caleb Pott or Pett, 1678, 9

Robert Cressy, LL.B., 19 (?)

Fr. Hughes, Esquire Bedell, 1633, 26

Th. Wood, (15..), 33

Edw. Hughes, (16..), 47

LIST OF OWNERS OF MANUSCRIPTS.

Monastic.

Durham Priory, 1, 6, 13–15, 20, 22–25, 28, 29, 35, 40, 41, 44, 45, 48, 50, (51–53), 54, (56), 57, 59, 61, (64), 65–71, 76

Durham College, Oxford, 29

Bury S. Edmunds, 18, 49 (?)

Blith, 19

Bathwick (?), 32

Hexham, 38

Kirkstall, 75

Praemonstratensians of (?), 55

Rievaulx, 34

Private.

Abingdon, Pet. de, 29

Alcok, 2

Andrews, 17

Audley, Th., 46

Barcroft, G., 74

Benn, J., 74

Blyth. G., 74

Bryston, T., 21

Carlyll, W., 10

Clyfton, Edm., 19

Collywood, W., 73

Cottrell, Mrs, 47

Cressy, Rob., 19

Doket, And., 27

Driffeld, Jo., 75

Ffysshburn, Jo., 61

Grindall, Edm., 47

Gunthorp, Jo., 49

Hallughton, J. de, 41

Hamsterly, J., 61

Hanmer, D., 47

Hanmer, J., 47

Horsley, Rob., 41

Hughes, R., 17

Iveson, Th., 16

Knagges, Greg., 63

Low, Th., 4

Lutebyr, H. de, 68

Man, Th., 8, 73

SCRIBES.

INDEX.

CAMBRIDGE: PRINTED BY J. AND C. F. CLAY, AT THE UNIVERSITY PRESS.